Governors, Grants, and Elections

JOHNS HOPKINS STUDIES IN AMERICAN PUBLIC POLICY AND MANAGEMENT

Manuel P. Teodoro and David M. Konisky, Series Editors

Governors, Grants, and Elections

Fiscal Federalism in the American States

Sean Nicholson-Crotty

Johns Hopkins University Press
Baltimore

© 2015 Johns Hopkins University Press

All rights reserved. Published 2015

Printed in the United States of America on acid-free paper

9 8 7 6 5 4 3 2 1

Johns Hopkins University Press

2715 North Charles Street

Baltimore, Maryland 21218-4363

www.press.jhu.edu

Library of Congress Cataloging-in-Publication Data

Nicholson-Crotty, Sean.

   Governors, grants, and elections : fiscal federalism in the American states /
Sean Nicholson-Crotty.

      pages cm. — (Johns Hopkins studies in American public policy and
management)

   Includes bibliographical references and index.

   ISBN 978-1-4214-1770-7 (pbk. : alk. paper) — ISBN 978-1-4214-1771-4
(electronic) — ISBN 1-4214-1770-7 (pbk. : alk. paper) — ISBN 1-4214-1771-5
(electronic)   1. Federal government—United States.   2. Intergovernmental
fiscal relations—United States.   3. Grants-in-aid—United States.   I. Title.

   JK325.N55 2015

   336.73—dc23   2014047467

A catalog record for this book is available from the British Library.

Special discounts are available for bulk purchases of this book.
For more information, please contact Special Sales at 410-516-6936 or
specialsales@press.jhu.edu.

Johns Hopkins University Press uses environmentally friendly book
materials, including recycled text paper that is composed of at least
30 percent post-consumer waste, whenever possible.

Contents

Series Editors' Foreword

State government pursuit and spending of federal grants is supposed to be apolitical, at least according to conventional theories of fiscal federalism. Traditionally, scholars have assumed that governors will always seek federal grants, either in response to state fiscal demands or because the incentives embedded in the grants themselves make them difficult to turn down. From states' perspectives, federal money is "free money" after all—why not go after it? One might go as far as to say that, when it comes to federal grants, governors have been portrayed as "single-minded seekers of federal money" (with apologies to David Mayhew).

But this portrayal flies in the face of recent experience. When the U.S. Supreme Court ruled in 2013 that states could not be compelled to participate in the Medicaid expansion component of the federal Affordable Care Act, many governors around the country took the opportunity to opt out of the program. In so doing, they left on the table billions of dollars to help pay for the expansion of health coverage for the uninsured poor. Similarly, when the Obama administration created a high-speed rail program under the American Reinvestment and Recovery Act, several governors declined the new federal money to upgrade their rail infrastructure. That is, some governors around the country looked at billions of federal dollars placed before them and walked away.

How do we square these high-profile recent cases with the conventional wisdom on fiscal federalism? Are these examples exceptional, or do they reflect a larger phenomenon that scholars have failed to recognize and investigate? In this book, Sean Nicholson-Crotty provides a compelling challenge to the traditional view that the pursuit and spending of federal grants is an apolitical exercise. He develops and rigorously tests a new *political* theory of fiscal federalism that, at its core, argues that governors use the federal grant-in-aid system strategically to attain political objectives.

Nicholson-Crotty builds on existing theoretical perspectives of partisan and electoral politics to argue that governors solicit and spend federal public monies to deliver benefits to core constituents and then, as elections approach, to noncore voters whose support will improve reelection prospects for themselves and their copartisans. One of the novel features of Nicholson-Crotty's research is that he develops and empirically tests a unified theory that accounts for both the solicitation of federal grants and their expenditure, which the fiscal federalism literature tends to treat separately. His analysis goes a step further to address the important question of impact—that is, whether the spending of federal grants in a strategic and politically motivated way generates electoral benefits for incumbent governors and their parties.

Using mixed methods and an impressive array of empirical evidence, Nicholson-Crotty finds persuasive support for his core theoretical arguments. Studying federal grant programs of different types across varied policy areas and over several decades of time, he finds consistent evidence that governors are strategic in deciding which grants they seek and how they spend the money once it arrives in state coffers. Further, he shows that the strategic use of federal grants can provide electoral dividends. What emerges from his comprehensive analysis is a new perspective on fiscal federalism that is expressly political.

In developing and empirically testing his argument, Nicholson-Crotty connects what have been disparate literatures in electoral politics, federalism, and state politics, offering a powerful logic for understanding how politics shapes federal grants. Given the sheer scale of federal grant to states—which total tens of billions of dollars each year—these findings are consequential for understanding the intersection of politics, public policy, and public administration.

This book embodies our purpose in the Johns Hopkins University Press series, Studies in American Public Policy and Management. We encourage work that addresses contemporary American public policy and management issues with theoretically rich and empirically robust research. Books in the series take up public policy, politics, public administration, and/or public management. We proceed from the premise that public policy effectiveness is inevitably linked with public management and administration, and that public policy, administration, and management are irreducibly political.

Contributions to Studies in American Public Policy and Management generally center on the United States and on issues that are national in scope, but we are also interested in projects that deal with policy and management at the state and local level. Books in the series are written for a scholarly audience of academics and students but also have an eye toward application and relevance to policymakers and public administrators.

We hope the books in the series advance academic thinking while enlightening our understanding of how to effectively address pressing public policy and management challenges.

Manny Teodoro, Texas A&M University

David Konisky, Georgetown University

Acknowledgments

I have been studying the relationship between the states and the federal government, including the grant-in-aid system, my entire career. I have always believed that state governments exercise a great deal more agency in that relationship than they are given credit for and that this is an intensely political issue at the state level. In many ways, therefore, this book is a natural outgrowth of longstanding interests and beliefs.

Like many of my better ideas, however, this one was also sparked in part by a helpful suggestion from an anonymous reviewer. That person noted that while the topic of how states spend grant money was fine, it would be *far* more interesting (emphasis in original!) if it could be shown to influence other major features of the American political landscape. So in some ways, this project is an attempt to make the study of grants more interesting to a wider audience. I hope it offers a convincing account of the linkage between governors' decisions about grants and their popularity, legislative clout, and, ultimately, electoral success.

The University of Missouri was a great place to start both this project and my career. I am grateful to numerous members of the political science department there not only for providing feedback on much of the research that fills these pages but also for their advice on how to organize and write my first book-length project. I owe a particular debt of gratitude to Jonathan Krieckhaus, Cooper Drury, and Lael Keiser. I am also indebted to many graduate students whose thought-provoking discussions in my federalism seminars, herculean data collection efforts, and collaboration on papers and articles all contributed significantly to this final product. I particularly want to thank Mark Ritchey and Tucker Staley for all their hard work.

By the time I arrived at Indiana University, I had a draft of the manuscript completed and therefore assumed that the lion's share of the work on this book was behind me. Needless to say, this was hopelessly naïve. I am greatly indebted to my colleagues in the School of Public and Environmental Affairs for providing the resources, both intellectual and financial, which helped me to finish the project. Finally, and most importantly, I owe to my family more credit than can be squeezed into this brief acknowledgments section. My wife, Jill, provided the emotional support necessary to navigate the considerable risk and uncertainty that accompanies a project of this size. That in itself is an invaluable role. However, I also benefitted from the fact that my spouse is a powerful intellect and a prominent academic in her own right. As such, Jill also provided substantive feedback on almost every argument and analysis used to build the story herein, and the book is infinitely better for it. My kids, Finn and Iris, also deserve a lot of credit for helping me cope with the stress that sometimes accompanied this project. They remind me that I have already been luckier than I probably deserve, regardless of what becomes of my academic career, which is very relaxing.

Governors, Grants, and Elections

Chapter One

Introduction

On March 23, 2010, after a long and contentious legislative battle, President Barack Obama signed the Patient Protection and Affordable Care Act (PL 111-148) into law. The goals of the PPACA, or ACA as it is commonly known, were multifaceted, but its primary purpose was to reduce the number of uninsured and underinsured persons in the United States. Initially, the mechanisms within the law that received the most attention were those designed to achieve that goal among middle- and lower-middle-class Americans, including the individual mandate, state-level insurance exchanges, and new regulations on insurance companies and employers. Among the most consequential pieces of the ACA, however, was a mechanism designed to achieve the goal of higher insurance rates among America's poor. Specifically, the law mandated that all states expand Medicaid coverage to citizens below 138% of the federal poverty line, including nondisabled but childless adults. As passed, the ACA included harsh sanctions for states that failed to implement an expansion, including the potential loss of all federal Medicaid funds.

In order to offset the cost of the expansion for states, the law committed the federal government to pay 100% of the cost of new enrollees for the first three years and 90% each year after that until 2022. Medicaid is the largest federal grant to state governments, totaling $265 billion in 2012, and the federal match proposed to cover Medicaid expansion represented a large increase to that already enormous sum. The size of the increase is particularly easy to see in individual states. For example, it is estimated that Texas would receive an additional $9.6 billion in federal funding by 2022 in return for expanding Medicaid. Michigan is projected to receive an additional $2.5 billion over the same period. By comparison, this is more than twice the amount projected to be received by each state from the Highway Trust Fund.[1]

In 2013, the U.S. Supreme Court issued a ruling in *National Federation of Independent Businesses v. Sebelius* that significantly altered Medicaid expansion and the distribution of grant funding associated with it. In that decision, the Court famously upheld the constitutionality of the individual mandate and, in a less-heralded part of the ruling, declared that the Medicaid expansion was not a valid exercise of Congress's spending power. This, in essence, gave state governments the ability to opt out of Medicaid expansion, and immediately following the ruling several states declared their intention to do so. As of 2014, 24 states had failed to lower eligibility to the level mandated by the ACA and thus forgone the increase in federal grant funding associated with expansion.

From the perspective of this study, the most interesting questions are why some states chose to forgo billions in federal funding and what those choices can teach us about the U.S. grant-in-aid system more generally. A quick look at the states that initially opted out leads almost inevitably to the conclusion that the decision to leave billions in federal grants on the table was simply an extension of the bitter partisan battle that surrounded the ACA. Over 90% of the states that had chosen not to expand Medicaid by 2014 had Republican governors. Journalists called it the "final battle in war over Obamacare."[2] The president publicly expressed his frustration with "states that have chosen not to expand Medicaid for no other reason than political spite." Republican governors said it boiled down to the fact that "the majority of Americans no longer trust President Obama."[3]

In many ways, the recognition that partisan politics kept states from accepting billions of dollars in federal Medicaid grants is interesting enough to warrant our attention—a point we will return to in a moment. However, the real story of state decisions regarding the Medicaid expansion is more nuanced and potentially even more instructive. More than one-third of Republican governors *did* expand Medicaid and accept their share of increased matching funds.[4] And this was not just a case of liberal legislatures shoving expansions down governors' throats. In some cases, like North Dakota, governors were signing legislatively approved eligibility changes that they had championed. In others, like Ohio, the governor made controversial use of an executive Medicaid board in order to expand the program over the strident opposition of Republicans in the state legislature. Often, though not in every case, the Republican governors that expanded Medicaid faced very different reelection prospects than did their counterparts that had loudly declined Medicaid funds. On average they had won their previous election by a smaller margin of victory and were governing a citizenry that was significantly more liberal when compared with other Republican governors.[5]

Electorally "conflicted" governors on both sides of the political aisle tended to pursue increased federal Medicaid funds quite strategically. Both Democrats in relatively conservative states like Iowa and Arkansas, and Republicans in fairly liberal states like Pennsylvania, chose to expand Medicaid but did so under the aegis of 1115 waivers. Generally speaking, section 1115 of the Social Security Act allows the federal government to waive some requirements of federally funded programs in order to give states additional flexibility to design, and ostensibly improve, programs by better matching them with local needs. In the case of Medicaid expansion, waivers have allowed states to make fairly substantial changes to federal requirements such as offsetting higher Medicaid eligibility thresholds with premium assistance to affected groups. These waivers arguably allowed governors to secure the increase in federal grant aid with a policy that is somewhat more palatable to their constituents.

Thus a quick examination of Medicaid expansion suggests that state actors sometimes leave massive sums of federal grant money on the table for reasons that appear to be openly partisan. It also suggests that partisanship may play less of a role in the decision to accept increased grants when actors cannot depend exclusively on copartisans for reelection. And, finally, it highlights a key mechanism that governors use to win concessions from the federal government and adapt grant programs to state needs. In other words, it suggests that state actors use the grant-in-aid system *strategically* in order to maximize political and other goals. This is a significant departure from much of the literature on fiscal federalism and is the primary argument of this book.

A Political Theory of Fiscal Federalism in the American States

In this book, I develop and test a political theory of fiscal federalism in the American states. The primary argument throughout is that incumbents strategically utilize grant monies to increase the probability that they or their parties will retain control over policy-making institutions. The argument, which will be fully developed in the next chapter, draws heavily on theories of public expenditure that seek explanations for the variation or cycles observed in government spending. The first of these is *partisan theory*, which provides the primary theoretical foundation in this book. Partisan spending theory suggests, rather intuitively, that politicians produce policies and spend public monies in order to deliver benefits to their core constituents. The second theory of public expenditure considered is *electoral theory*. It suggests that, conditional on electoral security, incumbents spend public monies opportunistically as elections approach in order to increase support among noncore voters. This second perspective, often labeled as the "political business cycle," has received considerably less empirical support but is nonetheless considered as a potential framework for understanding grant-related behavior in the states. It is important to note that, regardless of the explanation for spending cycles, studies of partisan and electoral influences both assume that spending and policy decisions made by incumbent politicians are designed to help them or their parties retain power.

Applying these theoretical perspectives to the pursuit and expenditure of federal grants in the American states assumes, of course, that state-level politicians have some discretion in the character of funds they receive and the ways those funds are spent once they enter state coffers. Fortunately, the existence of such discretion has been demonstrated repeatedly in the fiscal federalism literature.[6] So with that assumption met, partisan and electoral theories of government spending can guide us to a set of expectations about the use of federal grants by state actors.

Partisan theory suggests that members of both parties will, when they are able, solicit and spend federal monies in order to produce policies that appeal to core constituents. This expectation rejects the common wisdom that states will take whatever federal money they can get either because of fiscal need or because of universalistic incentives built into grants.[7] Instead, it expects that state politicians will apply for and spend grants for the same reason that federal politicians create and award these funds—to repay the loyalty of core constituents in previous elections and to mobilize them in future contests. Electoral theory, on the other hand, suggests the hypothesis that, when electoral security is low, state-level incumbents will use grants to capture the median voters because they lie outside of the core constituency. The theory offered here also acknowledges the possibility that partisan and political cycles may not be independent of one another and that state-level actors may use grants to satisfy copartisans unless high electoral uncertainty motivates them to opportunistically use federal monies to appeal to noncore voters. Ultimately, the assumption that governors, as rational actors, expect and receive some electoral benefit for themselves and their parties from the strategic pursuit and expenditure of federal grants underlies the application of partisan and electoral spending theories to the question of grants in the states.

Chapter 2 develops this theoretical approach more comprehensively and identifies specific testable hypotheses regarding the pursuit and expenditure of federal grants by governors as well as the conditions under which grants should produce an electoral payoff for incumbents and their parties. It justifies the focus on governors, arguing that these are state-level actors that are best positioned to take strategic advantage of federal funds. The chapter also develops the argument that the ability of state executives to convert grants into political resources is constrained by a number of institutional and contextual features of state government and specifies the conditions under which we should be most likely to see governors strategically pursue and spend grants. Finally, it draws on interviews with agency personnel, members of governor's administrations, and state legislators from a sample of states to establish the plausibility of the political theory of fiscal federalism in the American states.

Testing the implications of the theory outlined in the next chapter is challenging for a variety of reasons. The first of these is observability. Applying for grants in an attempt to garner reelection may seem untoward and is something that incumbents are unlikely to admit. Though we know that reelection is among the key determinants of elected officials' behavior once in office, it is often difficult to get politicians to admit that their choices are driven by an electoral motivation.[8] Even more challenging is that the diversion of federal funds from targeted programs in order to reward core constituencies or to court noncore voters creates the possibility of adjudicative action by federal agencies and puts the continued receipt of grant funding at risk. Obviously, these risks provide considerable incentive to obscure such behaviors from view.[9]

Other problems in testing the political theory of fiscal federalism are perhaps less challenging than these observability concerns, but they are nonetheless worth noting. The first of these is the breadth and range of hypotheses generated by the theory. Previous work on fiscal federalism has typically been concerned with the receipt and distribution of grants-in-aid or the expenditure of those grants by recipient jurisdictions.[10] Theoretical work such as Volden's,[11] which acknowledges that these are both integral components of the same institution, has not empirically tested expectations about state behavior in both the pursuit and the expenditure of federal grants. This book is novel, therefore, in that it suggests that a single motivation can explain a range of fiscal federalism behaviors by state actors.

The focus on partisanship as a key motivation raises its own challenges. This is because, obviously, a Democrat from Vermont and a Democrat from Alabama are likely to have different preferences. Political ideology is certainly more comparable geographically, and scholars have demonstrated that ideology predicts differences in the way grants are spent by state-level actors.[12] The key argument in this book, however, is that governors use grants for electoral advantage and that elections in the United States are inexorably intertwined with political parties and the outcomes that voters attribute to them. As such, party is the most theoretically appropriate variable, but the geographic variation in the positions and behaviors of political parties in the United States must obviously be addressed.

In response to the challenges mentioned above, this book adopts a mixed methods approach, employing both quantitative and qualitative data. In terms of the quantitative evidence, it is difficult to imagine a single dependent variable that could provide conclusive evidence for most of the hypotheses tested herein. For example, there is unlikely to be one model that could convincingly support the conclusion that partisanship influences the manner in which governors spend federal grant monies. In recognition of this fact, analyses in subsequent chapters model the many elements of grant-related decision making with multiple measures, data sources, and estimators across a variety of time periods and issue areas. This multifaceted approach provides numerous opportunities to "falsify" observed relationships and offers the best method for arriving at robust conclusions about a complex process. Whenever data are gathered over time, models include state-level fixed effects in order to ensure that results are driven by variation within a given state. This empirical strategy is central in addressing, among other problems, the geographic variation in U.S. parties.

When possible, the chapters augment statistical analyses with qualitative evidence. As noted above, semi-structured interviews are used to validate the plausibility of the theoretical framework that guides the book. The qualitative evidence provided throughout the remainder of the analysis varies in type and source. It is typically designed to offer confirmation of empirical results or to provide nuance and detail that quantitative data cannot, rather than to allow the reader to draw out of the sample inferences about the relationships it describes.

Turning then from challenges and solutions to actual tests of the theory, chapter 3 examines the politics of grant receipt by state governments. More specifically, it explores whether partisanship, electoral security, or the interaction of these factors influences the grants that governors apply for and receive. In response to the challenges outlined above, the chapter draws on multiple datasets, dependent variables, and methodological approaches. First, it investigates participation by states in discretionary grant programs offered by two federal agencies with identifiable preferences (DHHS and DOJ) on either side of a gubernatorial electoral cycle (2004, 2006, and 2008). Next, it explores the inflow of funds from six project grants between 1993 and 2005. It then provides both a quantitative and a qualitative analysis of the application process in the Race to the Top education grant competition that occurred during 2010. Finally, the chapter examines the pursuit by governors of waivers to federal requirements regarding the design of major formulaic grant programs. Specifically, it explores the impact of partisanship, electoral security, and the interaction of the two on 1915(c) Home Health Care waivers to the Medicaid Program between 1998 and 2008 and work requirement waivers to the Aid to Families with Dependent Children Program between 1992 and 1996.

Chapter 4 turns to the question of grant expenditure. Again, it marshals evidence from numerous datasets and analyses, both quantitative and, to a lesser degree, qualitative, to test the theoretical propositions outlined in chapter 2. First, it examines the relationship between grants and tax effort across all fifty states for the years between 1971 and 2005, looking specifically for the degree to which that relationship was moderated by partisanship, electoral security, and the interaction of the two. Next, the chapter isolates major distributive and redistributive grant programs in order to test the assertion that these types of funds should generate different levels of state spending depending on the political party that controls the governor's mansion and the electoral pressures faced by the governor. The chapter then examines State-of-the-State addresses in order to explore the types of grant expenditure decisions that governors claim credit for as well as the timing of those credit-claiming exercises relative to electoral cycles. Finally, chapter 4 explores an alternative expenditure decision by governors that might suggest the strategic use of grants in pursuit of electoral gain. More specifically, it investigates whether governors and their agencies spend more federal funds in the districts of legislative copartisans.

Chapter 5 examines the relationship between grants-in-aid and the electoral fortunes of incumbent governors and their parties. Specifically, it tests whether, ceteris paribus, grant revenue correlates positively with the vote share won by incumbent governors or their parties in U.S. gubernatorial contests between 1972 and 2004. It also develops and tests the argument that any relationship between grants and electoral fortune is likely to be moderated by the partisan conditions within a state. In order to increase confidence in the primary results, the chapter explores the relationship between grants and two antecedents of vote share, gubernatorial popularity and legislative success.

Finally, chapter 6 reviews the evidence for a political theory of fiscal federalism in the states provided throughout the book. It then draws some conclusions from that evidence and explores some potential implications for U.S. federalism.

Why Develop and Test a Political Theory of Fiscal Federalism in the States?

Before moving on, it is important to answer the why question. There is no shortage of research on state-federal relationships generally, and fiscal federalism specifically, so why spend time writing another book on the subject? The primary motivation for this project is that the existing literature does a very poor job of explaining the strategic grant-related behavior described in the opening vignette of this chapter. It has an equally difficult time explaining numerous examples of similar behavior, including the rejection of federal Emergency Unemployment Compensation (EUC) funds and high-speed rail grants by some Republican governors but not others during the Obama administration or the variability in Democratic governors' decisions to forgo Abstinence Education grants during the presidency of George W. Bush.

This gap in the explanatory power of current theory arises because, while we know a good deal about the politics of grant creation and distribution in the national government, we know very little about the degree to which political factors influence fiscal federalism in decision making at the state level. As far back as 1977, Edward Gramlich noted that the biggest barrier to understanding fiscal federalism in the United States was "the lack of an underlying theory of the behavior of state and local governments."[13] Unfortunately, we have not made a great deal of progress since then, particularly if we are interested in a *political* theory of state behavior. Obviously, what follows cannot be a comprehensive review of the literature on federalism or even on federalism in the U.S. context. Rather, it is a purposive sample of studies concerned explicitly with fiscal federalism and the relationship between state and national governments.

Studies of the U.S. federal government have demonstrated that grant allocations reflect shared party affiliations and are used to advance partisan agendas.[14] At its core, this research suggests that national actors use grants to buy or reward the support of voters, politicians, and interest groups in important jurisdictions.[15] Scholars have also provided evidence that grant type, as well as amount and recipient, is often manipulated by national politicians for political gain.[16]

Research on fiscal federalism from the state perspective looks quite different. Indeed, a good deal of the literature in this area portrays state-level decision making related to grants as essentially *apolitical*. Some of this work suggests that state governments have become so dependent on federal funds that—no matter how opposed they may be to the associated policy goals— they cannot realistically decline grants.[17] Another prominent body of work suggests that the most important decisions regarding the receipt and expenditure of federal grants are actually made by program administrators within granting and recipient agencies. This notion of "picket-fence" federalism envisions vertical linkages between these administrators (hence the fence metaphor) that allows functional rather than political concerns to dominate the grant-in-aid system.[18] Much of the literature on grant expenditure argues that the degree to which recipient jurisdictions spend grants in accordance with federal preferences is a function of the restrictions placed on the money by the national government or the degree to which it monitors states to ensure compliance.[19]

Of course, there is some work that acknowledges the political dimensions of state-level decision making regarding fiscal federalism, but it does not take us very far toward understanding the ways in which state politicians strategically utilize grants to achieve political goals. In one of the earliest of these studies, Richard Nathan (1983) offered a "predictive theory" of federal grants that sought to explicitly incorporate state and local politics. The theory predicts that the perceptions of a grant by subnational political "generalists" (i.e., governors and mayors) and the representatives of interest groups in a particular jurisdiction have an important impact on the ways in which funds are sought and spent. One of the key insights from work by Nathan and his followers was that these perceptions help to determine whether recipient jurisdictions replace own-source funds with grants and that politically liberal jurisdictions were less likely to do so.[20] While these studies tell us that pro-spending governments (proxied with liberal ideology) are more likely to use grants to grow (rather than maintain) public goods production, they do not tell us if the politicians in these jurisdictions make these grant expenditure decisions to improve their electoral fortune or to maximize some other political goal.

As another example of work that has touched on the political dimension of grants at the subnational level, numerous studies have demonstrated that the demand or need for a public good within a jurisdiction—typically proxied with constituent characteristics—influences the amount of federal money it receives.[21] Presumably, satisfying these demands has an electoral payoff for local and state-level politicians, though this has not been explicitly tested. Moreover, in these models, politicians are treated as more or less perfect delegates, seeking grants only to the degree to which the average constituent wants the program or service provided by those funds. There is little room for political actors to manipulate grant receipt or expenditure to maximize their own utility. These models do a poor job of explaining things like the recent High-Speed rail controversy in Florida, where governors representing the same set of constituents reached very different conclusions about the "appetite" for federal funds within their state.

A small number of studies have also examined the degree to which constituent characteristics help to determine the expenditure of federal monies. This work suggests that grants will have a larger stimulative effect in jurisdictions where citizens share the preferences of the national government regarding the policy, regardless of the restrictions placed on the money or the level of monitoring.[22] Other research in this vein shows that constituent characteristics can influence, albeit moderately, the degree to which shifts in federal funding are able to drive changes in policy priorities within a jurisdiction.[23] Again, however, while they make progress toward a political explanation of state behavior, these studies are incomplete because they treat constituent characteristics as a perfect proxy for the preferences of political actors within a jurisdiction, thus allowing no strategic variation in the behavior of those actors.

Theoretical work in "competitive federalism" probably takes the most explicitly political approach to fiscal federalism. It distinguishes between "functional" federalism—where decisions regarding the production of public goods by each level are driven primarily by capacity—and "legislative" federalism—where those decisions are driven primarily by the desire for electoral credit.[24] Paul Peterson, the primary architect of the approach, ultimately concludes that functional and electoral realities lead state governments to focus on the production of developmental policies (highways, education, etc.) because these are the ones that they are best able to produce and that are the most likely to garner an electoral payoff from budget-minded state-level constituents. Alternatively, he suggests that states rely on the national government, through the grant-in-aid system, to produce redistributive policies because of the greater fiscal capacity of the latter and because state-level voters are less likely to reward significant own-source expenditures on such policies. Ultimately, then, the predictions of early work in competitive federalism end up being surprisingly apolitical, driven by the institutional features of state governments (e.g., balanced budget rules), rather than by the partisan preferences or electoral goals of the people elected to run those governments.

In a formal extension of competitive federalism theory, Craig Volden's model allows strategic action among *both* national and subnational actors as each competes for electoral credit for the production of public goods. The federal government is the first mover in a noncooperative game when it decides to produce and then whether to produce independent of state effort or to incentivize state production. States respond to these decisions, deciding the quantity of the good they wish to produce independently, whether or not to accept a grant offered by the federal government, and the amount of the good to produce in response to accepted grant funding.[25] The real contribution of this model is the assertion that a state's behavior in the grant-in-aid system will be driven in part by its desire to claim electoral credit. The model is based on the foundational assumption that citizens know which level of government provides the public goods they demand and award credit accordingly.[26]

These recent extensions of competitive federalism theory are a step in the right direction both because they explicitly consider the electoral motivations of state-level actors and because they attempt to describe both the receipt and the expenditure of federal grants. They also have several shortcomings, however. First, the empirical evidence for the model is quite mixed. For example, studies have demonstrated that state-level politicians spend grant money as if they can *steal* electoral credit for the public goods produced with federal grants.[27]

The second shortcoming in recent models of competitive federalism is that they explicitly neglect the potential impact of partisanship. Work on the national government suggests that partisanship is a key determinant of grant-related decisions at that level, and there is little reason to believe that party does not also play an important role in the political calculations of state politicians.[28] Additionally, the neglect of partisanship impedes the ability of existing models to explain some recent fiscal federalism decisions in the states. For example, several of the governors that rejected Abstinence Only funds during the 1990s led relatively conservative states where a nontrivial portion of the constituency was supportive of the policy. As noted above, however, the president that championed the grant was a Republican and all the governors who turned it down were Democrats. Thus, it seems as if partisan politics likely played some role in these decisions.

One final emergent theory of state-federal relationships deserves some attention. In the past decade or so, proponents of "executive federalism" have suggested that the scope and character of federal programs implemented in the states is increasingly determined, not by eligibility and benefit decisions made by state legislatures, but rather by the implementation discretion sought by governors and granted by federal agencies.[29] For the purposes of this study, the theory of executive federalism is interesting for two reasons. First, it suggests that governors can have a meaningful impact on the amount of formulaic grant funding coming into their states and, equally importantly, on the ways in which states have to respond to those dollars with own-source spending. Because more than 80% of federal grants are distributed through the eight largest formula-driven programs, this is obviously a meaningful insight. Secondly, executive federalism is noteworthy because it acknowledges the significant variation in the political preferences of governors who seek waivers from federal agencies, and thus it can be classified among the growing number of theories attempting to incorporate politics into state-level perspectives on fiscal federalism.

Implications of the Theory

An explicitly political theory of fiscal federalism in the states like the one offered by this book has the potential to shed light on two of the most significant and frequently studied features of state-national relationships in the U.S. federal system. The first of these is the growth in national power vis-à-vis the states over the past century and, more importantly, the normative implications of that apparent centralization of authority. The second is the actual impact of federal grants-in-aid on state spending and the ultimate effectiveness of grants as a policy tool. As an externality of sorts, examining the relationship between the second-largest source of revenue in the states and the electoral fortunes of the politicians that manage those funds may also shed light on a less-studied dimension of U.S. federalism—the impact of that institution on subnational elections.

Safeguards of State Authority

The relative power of states versus the national government in the United States is perhaps the oldest and most fundamental question in the study of U.S. federalism. There has always been a normative element to this debate, with some suggesting that the central government should be the locus of greater authority and others arguing that a decentralized distribution of power is more appropriate.[30] Interestingly, for proponents of both positions, a primary concern has always been the muting of individual liberties and preferences. Advocates of more centralized authority suggest that national governments are better at preventing the "majority tyranny" that often represses individual rights in small homogenous societies.[31] Similarly, those who prefer decentralized authority have long argued that smaller states with more proximal governments are better suited to accommodate, and therefore less likely to restrict, the variation in political and social mores found within a citizenry.[32] An important element of this debate focuses on original constitutional design. Here there is considerable evidence and agreement that even staunch proponents of national power desired and designed a republic in which state governments retained significant (if not predominant) authority.

This general debate over state versus national power underlies two dominant streams of the federalism literature. The first of these focuses on the degree to which the balance of power between the levels has changed over time. For the most part, this literature has argued convincingly that national power has grown dramatically vis-à-vis the states, particularly since the turn of the twentieth century. As evidence, scholars point to the many preemptions, partial preemptions, mandates, direct orders, tax sanctions, and other policies limiting the authority of the states passed by the federal government during that period as well as to the dramatic expansion in the grant-in-aid system.[33] Authors have offered numerous explanations for this growth in national power, including the decline of state and local party organizations, the growing power of interest groups seeking national solutions to previously localized problems, the failure of states to overcome the collective action problem and mount an adequate defense against national intrusion, and the fact that federalism is a secondary value for national politicians from both parties when compared to more specific policy related preferences.[34]

In recent decades, there has been a good deal of political rhetoric about, and a corresponding uptick in scholarly attention to, the devolution of authority back to the states. However, conclusions from this literature suggest that, with the notable exception of welfare reform, the phenomenon was not as widespread or as significant as the rhetoric would suggest and that conservatives focused primarily on returning expensive and/or liberal programs to the states.[35]

The second stream of literature, underlain by normative concerns over the balance of power in the U.S. federal system as well as the recognition of a growing imbalance, deals with the need for "safeguards" of state power. The debate over safeguards has turned primarily on whether the Supreme Court needs to act as a defender of state sovereignty or whether the U.S. political system contains sufficient barriers to national encroachment. James Madison first articulated these "political safeguards" in *Federalist 46*, suggesting that the need to get elected by a constituency that has strong loyalties to state and local governments acts as a constraint on the willingness of national officials to encroach on the power of those governments. Legal scholars and jurists have found similar insights in the structure of the U.S. federal system. Herbert Weschler, who coined the phrase the "political safeguards of federalism," argued that members of Congress are selected in a way that is "intrinsically calculated to prevent intrusion . . . on subjects that dominant state interests wish preserved for state control."[36]

Not surprisingly, based on the proliferation of national policies that limit the authority of the states, many scholars have rejected the notion of political safeguards. They argue that whatever constraints may have existed in the eighteenth, nineteenth, and early twentieth centuries (i.e., selection of senators by state legislatures, strong state party organizations, etc.) have largely disappeared and that the Court has become the last line of defense for state power.[37] Some work has criticized "judicial safeguards" as thinly veiled conservative activism, but this work does not suggest that significant political barriers to national encroachment exist.[38] Similarly, other studies have suggested that there may be intermittent political safeguards of state power corresponding with national election cycles without contesting the general erosion of that power over time.[39]

We can return now to the question of a political theory of fiscal federalism in the states. Such a theory has significant implications for the debate regarding the balance of state versus national power discussed above. If it turns out that state-level electoral and partisan preferences have a significant influence on the pursuit and expenditure of grants-in-aid, then the role of these monies as a force for policy centralization and national government power must be reevaluated. At the very least, such a finding would suggest an alternative "political safeguard" of state power that has not been previously considered. More specifically, it would suggest that the ability of the federal government to encroach on state sovereignty via the grant-in-aid system is moderated significantly by the degree to which state actors see political advantage in allowing such encroachment. For advocates of state power, this will certainly be viewed as an unqualified good, but those with concerns about the sometimes repressive nature of homogenous state governments will likely reach a different conclusion. Regardless of the normative conclusions, a political theory of fiscal federalism in the states holds the promise of considerable empirical insights into the balance of power between the levels of the U.S. federal system.

The Impact of Federal Grants

Though not as storied perhaps as the debate over state versus national power, persistent questions regarding the substantive impact of federal grants-in-aid on state policy have been an important part of the federalism literature for the better part of fifty years. The recognition of partisan and electoral factors in grant-related decision making in the states also has the potential to offer some answers to these questions.

Most theoretically driven analyses of fiscal federalism have begun with a fiscal choice model and the assumption that grant effectiveness is a function of the number of restrictions placed upon the grantee. These suggest that more conditional matching or project-type grants would induce a greater expansion in recipient spending than unconditional lump-sum or formula grants.[40] The literature that tests these theoretical propositions has focused predominantly on the "flypaper effect" of federal grants, or the degree to which state (or local) money "sticks" to federal funds received by the jurisdiction.[41] Results suggest that the effect of a dollar of federal money varies wildly, motivating anywhere from 34 cents to more than $1.00 in own-source jurisdictional spending.[42]

Scholars have offered a variety of answers for the variability in the stickiness of federal money.[43] As noted above, a common answer for conditional grants has been the number of expenditure restrictions placed on the funding by the federal government. Other work on these types of grants suggests that the level of monitoring by the granting government has a larger impact on subnational spending than spending restrictions.[44] Empirical evidence that own-source funds also stick to unconditional grants has also prompted numerous explanations for jurisdictional spending decisions related to these funds. These include most notably the idea of "fiscal illusion," where grants convince unknowledgeable voters that public goods have become cheaper and increase their demand for them.[45] Others offer a "leviathan" explanation, suggesting that budget-maximizing bureaucrats and politicians use the complexities of the budgeting process to trick voters into allowing them to spend grants rather than return them as private benefits.[46]

Recent studies in this area have provided convincing evidence that conditions within a recipient jurisdiction have a significant impact on the stickiness of both conditional and unconditional federal grants. As noted above, some of this work demonstrates that the degree of citizen agreement with the goals of a grant help to determine the amount that lawmakers spend in the targeted area.[47] Other studies have shown that institutional features such as tax and expenditure limits affect the impact of grants-in-aid on jurisdictional expenditures, though they reach different conclusions about the direction of that impact. Particularly, germane to this study, Brooks and Smith suggest that cities with restrictive tax and expenditure limits must spend more of a grant in order to keep spending at the levels expected by the median voter.[48]

The perennial debate surrounding grant effectiveness, the large demonstrated impact of state-level ideological and institutional conditions, and speculation about an electoral explanation all speak to the need for a political theory of fiscal federalism in the states. Such a theory is unlikely to resolve the debate, but it may help to make estimates of grant effectiveness, which have remained widely variant despite decades of research, more precise by addressing what has likely been an omitted variables bias in previous work. Such a theory may also help to resolve recent disputes in this literature, clarifying why politicians facing the same institutional constraints spend more in response to grants in some cases and less in others. More specifically, modeling the electoral and partisan motivations of state actors can predict such behavior by illuminating the conditions when it is politically advantageous for them to supplement own-source funds with federal monies and those when supplantation is most politically rational.

A Better Understanding of State Elections

Finally, a state-centered political theory of federalism has the potential to offer insights into the factors that influence electoral success for governors and their parties. The research in this area has focused heavily on the impact of economic conditions on gubernatorial success but with mixed results. Early work, focused primarily at the election level, found little evidence of an impact for state economic factors on gubernatorial voting.[49] Alternatively, later work, focusing at the individual level, found an effect for both state economic factors on vote choice.[50] Importantly, this later work also demonstrated that sitting governors and their parties are held accountable by voters for increasing the tax burden. Federalism has been a consideration in previous work on gubernatorial elections, but it has primarily been used to test the rationality of voters in assigning responsibility for economic conditions.[51]

This book offers a different perspective on federalism and gubernatorial elections. The political theory of federalism does not suggest that governors are able to use grant funding to change macroeconomic conditions. It does expect, however, that they will apply for and spend grants in a way that allows them to provide public and private benefits to core constituents and, in times of electoral insecurity, to noncore voters. It explicitly rejects the assumption that underlies recent theoretical work on fiscal federalism—that is, that voters accurately assign credit for goods provision. Instead, it adopts an empirically verified alternative assumption that voters have very low information about policy-specific spending and that subnational politicians can, therefore, use federal grants to produce goods without raising additional own-source revenue and that they can claim electoral credit for doing so.

A Political Theory of Fiscal Federalism in the States

This chapter develops a theory of grants-in-aid as political resource for state-level incumbent politicians. More specifically, it outlines the ways in which state-level actors strategically utilize federal grants to deliver benefits to important constituencies and, as a result, help individuals and parties retain power in state-level institutions. The first step in this process is articulating the ways incumbents make decisions about the pursuit and expenditure of grants. The next is describing how these decisions can help them to secure reelection or maintain control of institutions. The third step in developing a political theory of fiscal federalism is identifying the state-level actors that are best able to take advantage of the electoral benefits of the grant-in-aid system, as well as the institutional and contextual factors that constrain their ability to do so. Finally, the chapter draws on interviews of state-level actors in order to explore the validity of some of the theoretical propositions laid out in the following pages.

The theory developed in this chapter rests heavily on the assumption that grants, responses to them, and the political consequences of those actions can be understood as conceptually similar to spending decisions. In other words, we can treat grants as revenue or potential revenue that elected officials decide to receive and then to spend on either public goods (i.e., government activities) or private goods (i.e., lower taxes).

A large and well-developed literature, much of which has already been reviewed, suggests that this is exactly how recipient jurisdictions conceive of federal funds. Sometimes, particularly in cases where they value the public good being provided, jurisdictions choose to treat grants as supplemental to their own spending. In this scenario grants have a price effect, increasing the quantity of a public good that the jurisdiction can purchase for the same level of taxation. This is the stated preference for almost every federal grant, whether it has an explicit matching requirement or not and, typically, grants do induce jurisdictions to purchase more of a public good than they would in the absence of federal funds. However, if there is ideological opposition to a program or significant income constraints, jurisdictions may use some portion of grant funding to replace own-source funds that would have been spent in the targeted policy area. In these cases, federal funds have an income effect, allowing jurisdictions to purchase the same amount of one public good, while simultaneously reducing taxes or increasing the purchase of *alternative* public goods.[1] The evidence suggests that the decision to supplant own-source spending with grants is not moderated very effectively by federal government efforts to influence state expenditure decisions.

The Medicaid program provides a good example of the sophisticated methods states have developed for converting even carefully monitored matching grants into income. A 1994 General Accounting Office investigation of the program in Michigan, Texas, and Tennessee concluded that "illusory accounting practices" had allowed these three states to secure over $800 million dollars in federal Medicaid grants without committing the required matching funds. In one instance in Michigan, the state made a payment of $213 million to the University of Michigan Hospital for the care of indigent persons. Because of the state matching rate in the state, that money was accompanied by $267 million in federal funds. Within hours, however, the University made an intergovernmental transfer (nominally unrelated to Medicaid) to the state government of $489 million, effectively allowing the state to receive the federal money with no accompanying state contribution.

The GAO reported that all three states were using similar transfers between the state government and state or locally run organizations to gain additional Medicaid funding. Interestingly, however, the report concluded that the states were doing different things with their ill-gotten gains. Texas and Michigan were using the money to finance increases in the cost of the Medicaid program without having to raise additional state monies, presumably through taxation. Tennessee was apparently returning the funds to the general operating budget, where they were presumably being spent on other programs.[2] Despite changes to the law in 1995 designed to limit the type of interorganizational transfers described in the 1994 report, another investigation in 2008 concluded that states were making billions of dollars in "supplemental payments" to providers as a new method for supplanting state funds with federal Medicaid dollars.[3]

The review thus far has focused almost exclusively on fiscal federalism in the U.S. context, but arguments there about the discretion of subnational grant recipients accord well with the larger literature on comparative fiscal decentralization.[4] That work consistently asserts that recipients of intergovernmental transfers have significant discretion, due to information asymmetries, in the use of grants. This discretion may be used to create fiscal illusion regarding the real cost of public goods, to lower tax effort, or to avoid tax competition with neighboring jurisdictions, among other things.[5]

States treat grants as revenue, which they choose to spend on targeted public goods, alternative public goods, or private goods for constituents. The primary research questions of this book concern why they make the receipt and spending choices they do with these monies, and when those choices can help them retain political power. We have reviewed a number of existing explanations for these decisions, but we will develop a fundamentally different argument in the following section. Drawing on political theories of state spending behavior, we suggest that state actors use the expenditure of federal grants to accomplish partisan and, ultimately, electoral goals.

Political Theories of Economic Policy and Outcomes

For obvious reasons, scholars have long been interested in the causes and correlates of government expenditure, monetary and fiscal policy outputs, and macroeconomic outcomes. This work has often focused on long-term changes in these patterns associated with the growth of the welfare state or on the corrections enterprise in developed economies.[6] Observers have also noted, however, that even developed economies show significant shorter-term fluctuations in spending and policy. Considerable attention has been dedicated to understanding this variation.[7] A prominent explanation for fluctuations in public spending and policy suggests that these factors vary cyclically over time, and authors argue that these cycles occur in response to partisan preferences, electoral pressures, or both. A review of these theories can offer insight into the receipt and expenditure of federal grant monies as well as the electoral payoff of those decisions. However, it is important to note that the literature on partisan and electoral cycles is massive and that the review presented below is but a small (though representative) sample of relevant work.[8]

The partisan theory of expenditure suggests simply that parties, when in power, implement policies that satisfy core constituencies. It is assumed that this "policy-seeking" behavior also helps parties retain power by solidifying their "brand" and mobilizing core voters in subsequent elections. The constituencies of left parties are assumed to prefer government expansion, while those who vote for right-leaning parties are assumed to favor contraction in the scope of government. More precisely, this work suggests that left parties cater to constituents that are more adversely affected by, and therefore have a stronger aversion to, unemployment.[9] Alternatively, right parties depend for support on upper-middle and upper class constituents who have relatively more to fear from inflation.[10]

The assumption that parties must satisfy the distinct preferences of their constituents leads to the expectation that they will manipulate monetary and fiscal policy as well as direct transfers in order to reduce either inflation or unemployment. Hibbs notes:

> Faced with demand shifts, supply shocks, labor-cost push, and other inflationary events, political administrations repeatedly have been forced to choose between accommodating inflationary pressures by pursuing expansive monetary and fiscal policies, thereby foregoing leverage on the pace of price rises in order to preserve aggregate demand and employment, and leaning against such pressures by tightening spending and the supply of money and credit, thereby slowing the inflation rate, at the cost of higher unemployment and lower growth.[11]

The empirical evidence for this expectation is fairly strong and relatively consistent across decades of research using different samples and employing methodologies that differ substantially in their sophistication. This work has found evidence of partisan effects on both monetary and fiscal policy.[12]

It has also demonstrated the effect of party on taxation, with right parties pursuing policies and tolerating outcomes that allow them to lower taxes.[13] Finally, authors have shown that there are significant differences in spending and transfer patterns across left and right governments, with left governments spending more and putting a greater emphasis on redistribution.[14] Despite theoretical expectations that they should, empirical studies have not found that party differences correlate strongly with larger budget deficits.[15] Research also suggests that partisan effects on fiscal and monetary policy are more easily observed in two-party versus multi-party systems and that the duration of the impact of party change on policies may be overestimated if voters are assumed to be adaptive and retrospective rather than rational and prospective.[16]

Electoral theory begins, not with the assumption that different parties must implement the economic policy preferences of their constituencies in order to retain power, but rather that all politicians are "office seeking" and act opportunistically as elections approach in order to achieve reelection goals. The earliest work in this area assumed adaptive, retrospective voters and office-seeking politicians and, from those assumptions, proposed that incumbent politicians could and would manipulate monetary policy in order alter economic outcomes and buy votes.[17]

Subsequent empirical studies found consistent evidence for the proposition imbedded within these models that incumbents have a higher chance of reelection when presiding over positive economic conditions.[18] However, the evidence for actual changes in economic outcomes corresponding to classic electoral cycles theory is extremely mixed.[19] Indeed, several comprehensive research programs completely reject the existence of a classic elections–outcomes relationship, at least in developed countries.[20] There is formal evidence that treating voters as rational and prospective (i.e., capable of foreseeing both elections and politicians' incentives), and thus dramatically reducing the information advantage enjoyed by incumbents over those voters, may help to increase the accuracy of predictions about the impact of electoral cycles on macroeconomic outcomes.[21] However, direct empirical tests of this proposition are relatively rare.

While it offers only the weakest support for the ability of incumbents to alter inflation or employment in order to enhance the prospect of reelection, scholarship on classic electoral theory offers better evidence that these actors manipulate *economic policies* in an attempt to do so. Tufte argued that incumbents have a variety of policy "weapons" beyond macro-level changes in inflation or employment that they can use to increase the likelihood of reelection. He suggested that they can target economic benefits such as benefit transfers, favorable tax policies (cuts or delayed increases), or public hiring at those voters needed to secure reelection.[22] He argued that, unlike macro-economic outcomes, these policy instruments are easily manipulable by incumbent politicians and can have an impact on recipients that is independent of the current employment/inflation balance. This assertion has received considerable empirical support in developed and developing nations, across national and subnational settings, and in numerous time periods.[23]

In sum, the large literature on political cycles offers several relatively consistent findings. First, it suggests that partisanship has a meaningful impact on economic outcomes and policy, with left governments pursuing higher employment and growth and right governments working to produce what is most valued by *their* core constituency—namely, lower inflation and taxes. The literature also suggests, albeit less consistently, that opportunistic behavior by office-seeking incumbents has an impact on economic policy as those actors manipulate transfer payments, public hiring, taxes, and other levers in an attempt to increase the chance of reelection.[24]

There have also been important extensions to electoral and partisan theories of economic policies and outcomes that should be noted before applying these to the question of fiscal federalism. Most germane among these is the notion of *conditional* electoral and partisan cycles. Franzese suggests that "the incentives for, capacity for, and effects of electioneering and partisaneering should vary predictably from policy to policy and across domestic and international, political-economic, institutional, structural, and strategic contexts."[25] In other words, the observable impacts of electoral and partisan cycles on economic policy and outcomes are highly conditional on the motivation for and ability of incumbents to manipulate these factors. In one of the earliest works on this subject, Tufte (1978) actually outlined several potential conditioning forces, including the closeness and importance elections, the division of policy-making authority among different institutions, and the relative strength of those institutions, partisan or ideological conflict among lawmaking institutions, and structural constraints imposed by previous decisions. Though this is certainly not an exhaustive list, the presence of numerous veto players with diverse interests, the existence of structural constraints such as debt limits, and the relative power of key policy-making institutions have all been shown to influence the impact of partisan and electoral cycles in subsequent empirical work.[26]

A second extension of the models reviewed above suggests that partisan and electoral manipulations of economic policy and outcomes might not be independent of one another. Frey and Schneider suggest that incumbents will pursue partisan goals, thus emphasizing policies preferred by core constituencies, only so long as their electoral future is relatively secure (i.e., public approval is relatively high).[27] As electoral uncertainty increases, however, they should be expected to move away from the ideological position and act opportunistically in order to increase overall popularity and the likelihood that they will capture the median voter in the next election. Though not perfectly consistent,[28] numerous studies have found support for Frey and Schneider's expectations.[29] A closely related argument suggests that ideologically and electorally driven manipulations of economic policy may exist at different times within the same incumbent administration. Alesina and colleagues suggest that left parties may pursue high-growth policies at the beginning of an electoral term but, recognizing that the resulting inflation will be electorally costly, may slow the rate of growth as elections approach.[30]

Though authors have suggested that "electoral security" might be measured with approval or election proximity, the empirical models of strategic grant use at the state level that appear throughout the remainder of this book will rely exclusively on the latter measure. This operational choice is necessitated by the inconsistent availability of approval data for state-level actors during the period under study.

Thus far, this discussion of the literature has focused exclusively on the politics of economic policy and outcomes. Underlying all of these investigations, however, is an assumption that incumbents expect some tangible electoral reward when they attempt to manipulate these variables. This expectation can be treated relatively quickly because the large literature on those payoffs offers fairly strong and consistent evidence. At the outcome level, there is clear evidence that, all else (like party) being equal, voters reward incumbent politicians for higher growth, lower inflation, and higher employment.[31] The modal study finds stronger evidence that voters reward or punish based on sociotropic rather than egotropic assessments, but there are numerous studies that find a link between individual economic well-being and vote choice,[32] which suggests that transfer payments that benefit specific groups can have a significant impact on electoral outcomes. There is also evidence of a link between popular economic policy and electoral success in national elections.

In the context of the American states, research suggests that poor economic conditions, tax increases, and reductions in individual economic well-being all contribute to a lower probability of reelection for incumbent governors and members of their party in the legislature.[33] Research has also suggested that levels of unemployment (both absolute and relative to surrounding states) influence the electoral success of incumbent governors or the nominees from their party. This is particularly true in cases of unified government, where voters can accurately ascribe responsibility for economic conditions.[34]

All of this suggests that the distinction between "policy-seeking" and "office-seeking" behavior in the production of economic policy and outcomes is somewhat contrived. Both types of actors can be treated as electorally motivated and interested in retaining power either for themselves or members of their political party. Opportunistic decisions meant to appeal to the median voter are obviously meant to achieve electoral ends. However, partisans who pass policies designed to satisfy core constituents are also doing so in part to maximize *electoral* utility or to increase the likelihood of mobilizing core voters in the next electoral contest. Indeed, research suggests that incumbents pay a clear electoral price when they *fail* to align their behavior with preferences of the constituents who put them in office.[35] This assertion is also consistent with work which recognizes that even incumbents who are easily classified as "policy seeking" have a desire to remain in office so that they can continue to promulgate the policies they and their constituents prefer. This desire grows from the related phenomena of "brand," or the policy image that parties try sell to voters in campaigns, and "issue ownership," or the set of policies that voters trust and expect a party to handle more effectively than their opponents. Research suggests that effectively marketing a policy image to voters and then delivering on the promises implicit in that image has at least a qualified influence on the electoral success of both candidates and parties.[36] Finally, the assertion that both types of incumbents are interested in retaining power also fits well with the work of Frey and Schneider and of Alesina and colleagues, which suggests that opportunistic behavior by incumbents only arises when electoral security cannot be achieved simply through the delivery of policies preferred by core constituents.

Applying Political Theories of Economic Policy to Fiscal Federalism in the States

Applying the insights discussed above to state-level decisions regarding fiscal federalism is relatively straightforward if we treat grant aid as a revenue source. In the most general (and simplified) case, grant-related decision making regarding that revenue is a two-stage process for incumbents. First, they decide which federal monies to apply (or qualify) for and accept. Second, they choose the proportion of federal funds coming into the state that will be spent on targeted public goods (e.g., better highways) versus the proportion that will be diverted to provide private benefits (e.g., lower taxes) or to pay for alternative public outlays. The first part of this section will apply the insights from partisan and electoral theories of spending to explain how much and what types of federal funds state-level incumbents receive and the choice of how to spend those monies. The second part will discuss the likely electoral payoff of grants-in-aid for state-level incumbents. Finally, the third part will discuss the institutional and structural characteristics of the state policy-making environment that are likely to condition electoral and partisan influences on grant-related decision making.

Grant Receipt and Expenditure

The decision by state actors to pursue and accept federal funds is their first opportunity to strategically pursue their goals via the grant-in-aid system. Describing the application for family planning funding, an aide to a midwestern governor said, "There were two pots of money, one for abstinence only education . . . and one for more complete programs. . . . We had to decide, 'Do we apply for one or both?' . . . The previous administration [Republican] had applied only for the abstinence only. We decided we would apply for both."[37]

Obviously, the degree of discretion that incumbents have in these decisions is dependent in part on the type of grant. State-level autonomy is highest in the case of project grants, which typically require an application from the recipient jurisdiction. In these cases, administrative and political costs, along (typically) with the accompanying own-source expenditures in the target area, represent the only real constraints on state decisions to pursue and/ or accept federal funds. Project grants constitute far and away the largest *number* of federal grants-in-aid, although they account for only about one-fifth of the *amount* of grant aid. Some prominent examples include the Environmental Protection Agency's Brownfields program, Health and Human Service's Family Planning Services, and the Department of Transportation's TIGER grant program. The Department of Education's Race to the Top competition offers another high-profile example of a project grant.

Formulaic grants, in which the level of federal funds is determined by the degree to which conditions in the recipient jurisdiction match those identified in statute, fall on the other end of the discretion spectrum. A large majority of federal grant funding is awarded through formulaic programs such as Medicaid, the State Children's Health Insurance Program, Highway Planning and Construction grants, and Title I compensatory education funds. Despite the fact that these grants are distributed in part on the basis of population, wealth, and other state characteristics written into the award formula, state policymakers still have a significant authority over the amount of money that their state receives from these programs. In the case of entitlement programs, which represent the largest category of formulaic aid, that authority comes through the determination of eligibility and benefit levels. For example, in the Medicaid/CHIP program, states make decisions regarding the income thresholds for eligibility (expressed relative to the federal poverty line), the eligibility of immigrant children, the eligibility of low-income working adults without dependent children, and the number of services eligible for program funds, among numerous others. For more concrete examples of this variation, note that states such as Wyoming do not provide state Medicaid coverage to children whose parent(s) make more than 100% of the federal poverty level, while Minnesota sets the threshold at 275%. Even after controlling for cost of care and matching rates, these choices have a significant impact on the amount of federal Medicaid funding that flows into a state. Moreover, as described earlier, states like Texas are choosing to reduce their allocation from a formulaic grant program by billions of dollars by choosing not to alter state-determined eligibility thresholds.

Some of the decisions discussed above are primarily legislative prerogatives, but research suggests that governors also influence inflows from formulaic programs like Medicaid because executive agencies play a role in determining which optional services a state offers.[38] Additionally, in cases like Ohio, boards appointed by the governor have an important role in benefit and eligibility levels. Executive influence is likely to be substantially larger in other formulaic programs, such as the Federal Aid Highway Program, where agency heads and program administrators are key actors in determining which projects are approved and, as a result, which federal dollars are committed to the state.

In addition to these avenues of influence, another source of gubernatorial control over formulaic funding flowing into a state is the waiver process. Sections 1115 and 1915 of the Social Security Act granted the president the ability to experiment with promising alternatives in the delivery of federally funding programming. Waivers of federal implementation guidelines, which are the primary vehicle through which this experimentation takes place, were originally targeted at programming that fell under the 1962 Act, but waivers to federal requirements are now granted in education, welfare, environmental, and a wide variety of other formulaically funded programs, in what authors have termed "executive federalism."[39]

Thompson and Burke suggest that "executive federalism emphasizes collaboration between the executive branches at the national and state levels to transform grant programs through the implementation process."[40] These and other scholars suggest that nowhere have waivers exercised greater influence on policy implementation than in Medicaid, the nation's largest formulaic grant program.[41] These authors have also intimated that governors are able to use the discretion inherent in Medicaid waivers to contain costs, expand services, and generally adapt the existing Medicaid program in a way that better fits the policy preferences of themselves and their constituents. Scholars suggest that this form of "executive federalism" has become an increasingly important source of state influence in recent decades.[42] In 2012 there were 460 active waivers to federal requirements granted by the Department of Health and Human Services (DHHS) alone across 19 different topic areas. At least one had been requested and secured by every state in the union.[43]

So with the recognition that state actors have considerable discretion in determining the federal funds flowing into a state, crafting a political explanation of grant receipt can begin with the insight from partisan theory. More specifically, it can begin with the insight that parties and incumbents maximize utility while in office by passing policies that appeal to core constituents. Key dimensions along which the core constituents of left and right parties in the United States differ is the appropriate size of government, the acceptable level of taxation, and, most importantly for this section, the types of policies that government should pursue. Research in the United States suggests that Republicans are more likely to invest the revenue they do spend on public goods in distributive policies that provide broad collective benefits

such as highways, law enforcement, natural resources, economic development, and education than on redistributive programs that provide particu-
larized benefits such as welfare, hospitals, and employment security.[44] The
vast majority of federal grants are explicitly intended to supplement, rather
than supplant, jurisdictional spending; and as such, receipt of such grants
implies the expenditure of some funds on the part of the jurisdiction.[45] Thus,
it is logical to expect that more federal money will follow the state funds that
governments are already spending or are willing to spend in a particular area.
Republican governments should receive more federal money from distributive
grant programs (e.g., education, highways, economic development, etc.) than
from grants targeted at redistribution (e.g., direct welfare payments, unemployment, public transportation, etc.). In a related argument, evidence suggests that right-leaning governments are willing to tolerate higher levels of
unemployment in order to maintain lower taxes and inflation and should
seek and receive less federal money targeted at enhancing employment.

Applying political theories of economic policy to grant expenditure decisions is equally straightforward, and here again we should assume that state
actors keep track of and are strategic about those expenditures. As the head
of an education agency from the Northwest noted, "There is the Office of
Financial Management in the Governor's office, and we have a liaison there
that we consult with. We usually don't have any trouble figuring out how to
spend the money, but we do interface with them to be sure it is in line with
what the Governor's team thinks is reasonable."

In order to generate predictions about what governors may think is reasonable, we can begin with the "truism" from the fiscal federalism literature
that state actors treat grant dollars as both a price reduction, allowing them
to purchase more of the targeted public good, and as income, which can be
spent on private goods (i.e., lower taxes) or other more highly valued public goods.[46] Obviously, the choice among these alternatives is constrained to
some degree by the restrictions put on funds and the degree of monitoring by the
federal government. Carefully monitored categorical grants provide low discretion regarding expenditure. Block grants such as Social Security, where funds can
be spent within a broadly defined program area, probably provide the most.
But the evidence is quite strong that recipients retain considerable discretion
over the expenditure decision regardless of grant type.

With these insights in mind, a partisan theory of expenditure would suggest that the choice to treat grant dollars as a price reduction or as additional

income is a function of the policy preferences of incumbents and their constituents. In other words, incumbents from both parties will spend grants in a manner that allows them to produce the outcomes that are most desired by core constituents or most consistent with their party's platform. As noted above, Republicans consistently campaign on the promise of less government spending and, as a result, a lower tax burden. This suggests that, all else being equal, incumbents from that party should be more likely to treat grant funding as income that can be diverted to citizens in the form of lower taxes and that grants will exert greater downward pressure on taxes in jurisdictions headed by Republicans. In the inverse, this implies that grants will have a larger impact on expenditures under Democratic incumbents, whose constituents are more likely to tolerate higher taxes and more government activity.

Because of differences in the preferences of core voters, partisan theory expects that grants in different policy areas will have varying impacts on own-source spending, depending on the party of the incumbent. Grants targeted at redistributive purposes or to enhance regulatory capacity within a jurisdiction should have a lower impact on spending in these areas under Republicans because of the distaste for these types of policies among Republican voters. Alternatively, grants for distributive policies (highways, education, economic development, etc.) that Republicans prefer should be used to purchase more of these goods than the jurisdiction could otherwise afford. This should produce a larger "flypaper" effect for these types of grants under that party. Finally, evidence that right-leaning governments are willing to tolerate higher levels of unemployment suggests that Republican incumbents may be more likely to supplant rather than supplement own-source funds with federal employment grants.

As noted above, the evidence for an electoral theory of economic policy is much weaker than it is for partisan cycles. However, scholars have offered some support for a "political-business cycle," approach, so it is important to acknowledge that electoral theory may also offer insight into grant receipt and expenditure decisions by state-level incumbents. As a reminder, that theory proposes that approaching elections provide an incentive to incumbents to act opportunistically, increasing transfers and improving economic conditions in order to maximize the likelihood of capturing the median voter in the next election.

Applying this proposition to the question of grant receipt suggests that the impact of opportunistic grant seeking should vary across policy area, depending on the party of the incumbent. The extensions of electoral spending theory discussed in the previous section imply that opportunistic economic policy behavior as elections approach is primarily meant to ameliorate the potential electoral costs of partisan policies and appeal to noncore voters. Similarly, increases in grant receipt during election cycles will be most useful if they appeal to voters outside the incumbent's core constituency and should therefore be most evident in areas not typically emphasized by each party. In other words, increases in grants for Democrats facing election should be greatest in highways, law enforcement, and so forth; while increases for Republicans should be largest in employment security, public transportation, and the like.

Electoral theory offers a related set of predictions regarding grant expenditure decisions. The basic model suggests that incumbents from both parties will use grants to purchase more public goods to increase support as the election approaches. The extension of the model discussed here suggests, however, that the types of goods purchased through this opportunistic behavior will vary depending on party. More specifically, it suggests that incumbents from each party will make grant expenditure decisions that appeal to the median (rather than their core) voter as elections approach. For Republicans, this implies that the predisposition to treat redistributive grants as income rather than to purchase additional social welfare will diminish. In other words, redistributive grants should have a larger impact on expenditures under Republicans running for reelection than under those who are not. Using these grants in the targeted policy area necessarily reduces the degree to which they can be diverted into private goods. As a result, the amount of grant funding used by Republicans to produce private benefits such as lower taxes should decrease during elections. For Democratic incumbents, opportunistic behavior during elections should mean that distributive grants have a larger impact on expenditures than they do during nonelection years.

The State-Level Electoral Payoff of Grants

The discussion above asserts that state-level incumbents will use grant aid strategically to maximize approval among core constituents during most of their term and then, if necessary, to leverage support from noncore voters as elections approach. If this is accurate, then it is plausible to assume that they expect some increase in the probability of reelection (or the likelihood of their party retaining power) to result from these manipulations. The partisan and electoral cycles literature suggests that this is a reasonable expectation, providing evidence that economic policy (e.g., debt reduction and tax cuts) and outcomes (e.g., lower unemployment) do correlate with the probability of reelection.

We expect, then, that state-level incumbents should also be able to use grants-in-aid to improve electoral security for themselves or their parties. Through either their price effect or their substitution for own-source revenue, grants can be used to reduce taxes; increase spending, growth, and employment; or provide transfer payments to key constituencies (depending on the party of the incumbent). When necessary, as in the case of low incumbent approval or high electoral competition, they can also be used to generate benefits for noncore voters who may be crucial to securing reelection. A higher volume of grant aid flowing into a state during an incumbent's term provides more opportunities to undertake these strategic manipulations and should therefore correlate positively with the likelihood of retaining power, all else being equal.

It is important to emphasize that grants are not expected to have an impact on elections independently, but rather through their impact on things that increase the popularity of incumbents and their parties. If this is the case, then we should also be able to observe a relationship between grants and approval. I expect that a higher volume of grant aid flowing into a state during an incumbent's term provides more opportunities to manipulate the influences on popularity and should therefore correlate positively with incumbent approval, all else being equal.

As has been noted throughout this discussion, the advantages of grant aid for approval and electoral fortune should accrue to parties as well as to individual incumbents. While campaigns in the United States are widely hailed as "candidate focused," there is also significant evidence of partisan effects on election outcomes. Furthermore, the related streams of research on political marketing and issue ownership suggest that what individual candidates accomplish, or more specifically the degree to which those accomplishments are in line with voter expectations for their party, helps to determine the future success not only of the individual but also of the political organization they represent. I assume, therefore, that politically motivated grant seeking and expenditure behavior by incumbents can help their party retain control of policy-making institutions even when they cannot run for reelection because of term limits or choose not to run for other reasons.

Governors are the state-level political actors who are best positioned to take advantage of the potential electoral payoff of grants-in-aid. However, it is important to give a bit more attention to the conditions under which the strategic use of grants is likely to have an electoral payoff for all state-level actors. These conditions turn on the partisan make-up of the electorate, reflecting the reality that a nontrival portion of vote choice is determined by partisan factors that are largely independent of public policy. This is what Fiorina identified as a partisan voting parameter, whereby some individuals vote for candidates from a particular party because of longstanding allegiances that often have very little to do with the current set of policies being championed.[47] This observation has been borne out empirically in decades of studies demonstrating a strong link between partisanship and vote choice even after controlling for the additive or moderating impact of other factors such as campaigns.[48] Traditionally, the consistent relationship between partisanship and vote choice has led to the assumption that there is relatively little room for the policy-specific activities of incumbents to influence the outcome of the next electoral contest for themselves or their parties.[49] Recent work has demonstrated a stronger role for policy in vote choice at both the individual and the aggregate levels, but these studies still emphasize that policy influence is conditional in important ways on existing levels of partisan identification.[50]

The most germane of these recent studies is Bertelli and John's (2013) work on the policy priorities of British governments over the past several decades. The authors theorize that, when in power, parties adjust their policy priorities to match those of the public, conditional on the expected value of doing so.[51] They demonstrate empirically that improved government "performance," measured as the accuracy with which a party adjusts its stated policy goals to match those of the public (given the strength of the public's desire for a policy and the risks associated with frequently shifting government priorities), correlates with higher vote share for the incumbent party in the next election. Most importantly for the purposes of this discussion, Bertelli and John demonstrate that the relationship between policy representation and electoral success is moderated by the partisanship of the electorate. Specifically, they show that positive impact of policy responsiveness *decreases* as partisan support for the prime minister's government increases. The explanation offered by the authors is quite intuitive: policy benefits "matter more when a larger compliment of swing voters is present" or, in other words, when the force of partisanship is weak enough to be overcome by those benefits.[52] Interestingly, the impact of responsiveness turns negative in those instances when the electorate is most unified behind the prime minister's party. Though the authors do not explore this possibility explicitly, this result may suggest that the government's constituency may be demobilized or disaffected in those cases where policy priorities seem tied to public whims rather than core party values.[53]

Bertelli and John's work suggests an important caveat to the expected relationship between grants-in-aid and incumbent vote share. I theorize that grants will be used to deliver policy benefits in hopes of achieving an electoral payoff. It seems reasonable to expect, however, that such a payoff may be moderated by the partisan context of the election. In other words, in those situations where a state politician is facing an electorate that is closely divided along partisan lines, grants-in-aid and the policy benefits they fund can produce a meaningful and observable increase in electoral support. Alternatively, in conditions where the electorate is overwhelmingly likely to support the incumbent because of shared partisanship, the marginal benefit of more grants is likely to be negligible.

Before moving on to a discussion of the state-level politicians best positioned to take advantage of grants-in-aid and the constraints on their ability to do so, it is important to refocus the argument momentarily. The literature on partisan and electoral cycles is a convenient and intuitive vehicle for developing some specific expectations about the ways state-level incumbents might strategically use and benefit from grants-in-aid. In the end, however, that discussion simply adds intellectual meat to the straightforward proposition that lies at the heart of this book—namely, that federal grants can be a political resource for state actors as well as for national politicians and parties.

Key Players and Constraints

It is natural to expect that incumbents in some states will be more successful than others in converting grant dollars into economic policies and outcomes that ultimately increase approval and electoral success. To understand that variation, it is first necessary to understand the political actors within a state that are best positioned to manipulate and benefit from the grant-in-aid system as well as the unique institutional and environmental constraints faced by those players.

Governors are in the best position to strategically utilize the grant-in-aid

system for partisan and electoral benefit in large part because of their influence over the priorities and actions of administrative agencies. The majority
of grants made to states are applied for by, awarded directly to, and/or administered by administrative agencies within that state. Indeed, agencies typically have significant internal capacity to undertake this endeavor in the form
of offices or departments dedicated to grants administration. In the case of
project and competitive grants like the Race to the Top, agencies initiate and
manage the application process through these offices. In the case of formulaic grants, such as those distributed though the Federal Highway Trust Fund,
state agencies continue to have enormous influence, through the project
planning process, over how much federal funding comes into the state and
the ways in which it is spent. When federal funds are partially tied to benefit
and eligibility thresholds, as they are in the major entitlement programs such
as Medicaid, state agencies influence the receipt and expenditure of funds
via their influence over program characteristics and providers.[54] Even when
funds are simply being "passed through" the state government on their way
to local jurisdictions, as in the case of the Community Development Block
Grant program, state agencies retain significant control by administering
competitions to determine which local projects receive funding.[55]

The role that state-level bureaucratic agents play in the grants process
puts governors in the best position to benefit politically from the grant-in-aid
system. Evidence suggests that governors can exert significant control over
agencies relative to other institutional actors due to their oversight capacity and that this influence has increased markedly over time.[56] Research also
suggests that gubernatorial priorities become even more influential in agency
decision making when governors are popular and/or have significant formal
and informal powers at their disposal.[57] This authority varies considerably
across states, but when exercised it allows governors to manipulate the grant-
in-aid system both by determining the amount of state funding that agencies
can use to leverage federal funds and by signaling gubernatorial preferences
regarding the receipt and expenditures of those funds to agencies.

In addition to their influence over agency behavior, governors are best positioned to use grants-in-aid strategically because of their considerable influence over the budgetary process. As a senior member of a midwestern education agency put it when referring to the relative power of the legislature and
the governor, "Even though they are both technically on equal footing, the

governor has a real advantage when it comes to using grants politically. He is responsible for preparing the budget."

Beginning in the 1950s, scholars argued that state executives dominated budget making because of superior institutional capacity relative to legislatures.[58] In recent decades, studies have theorized that gubernatorial influence may be slipping, but empirical tests suggest that on average governors continue to have greater influence in the appropriations process than do their legislative counterparts.[59] Fiscal analysis capacity in legislatures has increased significantly over the past 30 years,[60] but Budget Offices and/or Offices of Financial Management within the executive appear to have kept pace with this growth.[61] The most recent work in this area by Kousser and Phillips confirms that governors are successful in realizing their budgetary goals a very high percentage of the time.[62]

Thus, the extant research suggests that governors enjoy significant success in securing relative allocations (if not always absolute dollar amounts) for executive agencies that match their policy preferences. This level of influence over the awards to bureaucratic agencies is important to this discussion because federal grants and the dollars from the state that are supposed to accompany them are almost always included within the budget requests for specific agencies. In most states, the legislature will appropriate a total amount that an agency may spend during the budget cycle, including federal grants, the appropriate matching or Maintenance of Effort (MOE) funds, and independent state funds. The specific grants included in that total and the programs they fund are, in most cases, better understood by the agency, the Budget Office, and the governor than by the legislators voting on the budget.[63]

Despite the advantages they enjoy relative to other institutional actors, there are also significant constraints on governors' ability to convert grants-in-aid into political resources. One of the most significant of these is the level of formal power that a governor possesses. Among the most prominent of these is power over the budgeting process, and this varies dramatically from state to state, depending on whether the governor shares authority with the legislature for proposing the budget, whether agency budget requests go through the governor's office or directly to the legislature, and the presence of the line-item veto for legislative changes to the budget, among others.[64] Gubernatorial appointment power is also highly variable across states, depending on the number of agencies to which the governor can appoint a head and whether those selections require confirmation by one or more chambers of the legislature.[65] Because of their impact on administrative control, legislative success, and the general direction of state policy, it is reasonable to expect that governors with fewer formal powers will have a more difficult time utilizing the grant-in-aid system to their advantage.

A closely related but nonetheless distinct constraint on that ability likely arises from the institutional structure of the executive branch. In some states key executive offices (e.g., lieutenant governor, attorney general, auditor, etc.) are directly elected rather than appointed by the governor. Research suggests that this arrangement significantly dilutes the power of the top executive and reduces his or her ability to influence administrative agencies and the course of policy within a state.[66] All else being equal, the structure of the executive branch should therefore condition the ability of governors to strategically utilize grants-in-aid for partisan and electoral gain.

Of course, the biggest potential constraint on governors who seek to use grants-in-aid in this way is the legislature. Proposed agency budgets must ultimately be approved by that body as must any programmatic changes (e.g., addition or removal of Medicaid services) that agencies may make in response to gubernatorial priorities.[67] While the evidence is somewhat mixed, research also suggests that legislatures do, under some circumstances, effectively oversee and control agency decisions like those related to grant expenditure.[68] This is likely to be particularly true for very large or very controversial programs. As a deputy commissioner of health in a southern state reported, "They [the legislature] usually don't pay much attention to individual grants. There are times, however, when we've had to answer some questions about funding sources, for example, the ACA. They started looking at programs that didn't get much scrutiny before that." Finally, any changes that governors wish to make to economic policy in response to grants-in-aid, such as tax reductions, require the approval of the legislature. So while the state executive may enjoy an advantage in the area of fiscal federalism, it is obviously important to account for legislative preferences in any examination of the strategic use of grants-in-aid by governors.

A large literature has developed around the question of when governors are more and less successful at overcoming the legislative constraint inherent in a separation of powers system. Factors shown to contribute to executive success in the legislature include nearness to previous election (i.e., the "honeymoon" period); formal budgetary, appointment, and veto powers; and public approval.[69] Not surprisingly, being from the same political party as the leaders of one or both of the legislative chambers is among the most consistent and substantive predictors of an executive's ability to realize his or her policy goals.[70] Interestingly, and somewhat counterintuitively, recent work in this area has also demonstrated that governors may enjoy greater success in more professionalized legislatures.[71] Taken together, this body of work suggests that divided government, popular support, and the institutional features of both the legislature and the governor's office will condition the degree to which governors are able to strategically use grants-in-aid for political purposes.

Establishing the Plausibility of a Political Theory of Fiscal Federalism in the States

As has already been noted, the expectations produced by a political theory of grant-related decision making by governors are hard to test rigorously by simply asking the actors (or their surrogates) about motivations. Questions like, "Did the administration divert federal funds away from targeted programs?" or "Does the governor strategically manipulate the grant-in-aid system for electoral gain?" are unlikely to elicit accurate responses. Subsequent chapters thus make use of a great deal of quantitative data drawn from numerous disparate sources and analyzed in diverse ways. I occasionally cite publicly available qualitative accounts such as governors' State of the State addresses in order to corroborate the results from statistical analyses, which are the modal analytic technique in the rest of the book.

It is possible, however, to use qualitative data to explore the validity of at least some of the theoretical propositions offered throughout this chapter. In what follows I use interviews with state-level officials to address the plausibility of some of the key elements of the political theory of fiscal federalism outlined in this book. These interviews provide insight into questions of whether governors pursue grants to help them keep policy promises made to those that elected them, opportunistically pursue grants to capture noncore voters, have influence over which grants an agency chases and how those monies are spent once they come into the state, and, finally, have an advantage over other state-level actors in the strategic use of grants.

The interviews discussed below are drawn from a purposive sample of states and positions. I employed a rough approximation of a least-similar systems design to identify four states that differ on some of the major factors that might be expected to influence the interface with the fiscal federalism system, including region, party of the governor, presence of unified government, and level of dependence on federal grant aid.[72] Within each of those states, I sought to interview the federal liaison within the governor's administration, the director or deputy director of three executive agencies, and three state legislators. Ultimately, I was able to conduct a total of fifteen interviews, with at least three in each target state.[73] These include three members of gubernatorial administrations, eight administrators, and four state legislators. Again, it is important to note that these individuals are not a representative sample of like actors across the nation. If, however, these disparate sources consistently confirm the plausibility of the theoretical story outlined in this chapter, then we can have more confidence that expectations produced by that story are reasonable and that the empirical relationships discussed throughout the rest of the book present an accurate picture of state-level fiscal federalism in decision making.

At the heart of that story is the assertion that governors use grants-in-aid strategically in order to bolster their electoral fortunes. One way in which such strategic behavior may manifest is primarily partisan in nature, where "policy-seeking" incumbents use grants to produce public goods that are in line with the policy goals of co-partisans in their constituency. This assertion is not consistent with the common wisdom about states and grants, which holds that financially constrained governors take whatever money the federal government has to offer; however, its veracity was confirmed repeatedly in the interviews of state-level informants. Every one of the officials I interviewed responded yes to the question of whether the governor uses grants-in-aid to help him or her achieve policy goals. Indeed, the federal liaison from one midwestern state replied, "Undoubtedly." The director of a health agency from a western state used the word "Absolutely" instead. The individual in charge of state-federal relations from the same western state said simply, "The grants we apply for follow the governor's priorities for the state."

In only one case, did a respondent seem to indicate that more money of any flavor was the governor's priority. Specifically, a federal relations administrator from the Department of Transportation in a western state suggested: "It may not be the same way as with other agencies. The real policy goal in transportation is accelerated project delivery. The governor's—probably every governor's—priority is to get the project done and find any money that can help us do that." Interestingly, though, he did go on to say that "each of those projects has a policy goal which has to be signed off on by the commission, and they are appointed by the governor."

Other respondents almost always described policies that can be easily identified with one party or the other when giving examples of the types of grants pursued by their governors. For example, informants from departments of education in two states with Democratic governors both touted the pursuit of early childhood education funding. Alternatively, a deputy commissioner for education in a Republican-led state emphasized that the governor's education goals and the agency's strategic plan focused on funding for "new teacher evaluation initiatives . . . a database available to educators and non-educators that will allow anyone to dig down all the way to the teacher level, and [the] goal to revamp teacher licensure."

When asked for an example of the types of grants the Democratic governor had pursued, the deputy director of a midwestern health agency noted: "The summer food initiative is a good example. It was a backpack program targeted just at [city names excluded], I think . . . though it may have been the whole state. The governor was really interested in improving nutrition for inner city kids. We got a special grant and worked very closely with his office in the process."

All in all, the interviewees provided strong and consistent support for the assertion that governors pursue partisan policy goals via the grant-in-aid system. Evidence of opportunistic behavior, where governors use grants to appeal to noncore voters as elections approach, was far more mixed. Not surprisingly, the vast majority of agency personnel and federal liaisons answered in the negative when asked if the governor who appointed them "sometimes pursues grants to fund policies that might appeal to voters from the other party." The typical response resembled that of a midwestern education official who said, "There is an expectation that we work to capacity for the kids of [state excluded], and that drives our day-to-day operations." In one exception to that pattern, the director of the Department of Corrections in a Republican-controlled state claimed: "There are some things that we've experimented with that definitely drew some criticism. They probably would've been more difficult to pull off if we were asking taxpayers here in [state excluded] to foot the whole bill."

Generally, legislators from the governor's party were also hesitant to suggest that the executive used grants to capture voters from the other party. I was only able to interview two legislators from the opposing party, but this group was less sanguine about the lack of opportunistic grant behavior. One representative from a northeastern state said, "Probably," but was unable to offer any specific examples. However, an opposition senator from a southern state responded: "Now that I think about it, maybe. Agencies occasionally come to us for support on applications that they think we'd be interested in. It could just be a coincidence I guess, but it seems like we've gotten more of those this year." The governor of the state in question was seeking reelection in the year this interview was conducted.

Of course, the argument that governors "use" grants-in-aid strategically as policy maximizers and perhaps as electoral opportunities is less compelling in the absence of evidence that they actively coordinate with agencies regarding the pursuit and expenditure of federal monies. Fortunately, the officials interviewed for this study provide such evidence. All agency personnel and two of the three federal liaisons with whom I spoke suggested that such coordination is common, though it appears to take different forms. In several cases, informants relayed examples of direct involvement by the governor in a grant application. An education official from a northeastern state said, "I can only speak for the time that I have been working for the department, but in the past year there has been a great deal [of coordination]." A federal liaison from a western state suggested even greater involvement on a host of fronts:

> Particularly as new governors turned away rail dollars, we went after them. The governor has made a rail corridor into [city redacted] a high priority. We were also a strong proponent of the Affordable Care Act, and the governor aggressively went after the exchange grants. We were actually the [number redacted] state to receive one of the large awards. We were not successful with the K–12 Race to the Top application, but we were successful in the area of early childhood education. The governor actually created a department of early learning, and the grant was a real validation of [gender redacted] work.

Another federal liaison told a similar story of active coordination, asserting that "we require all departments to coordinate applications. . . . They identify them [grants], then I do quality control on the back end. . . . When there is a policy question about applying for the grant, they bring those to me up front, before putting together the application. . . . The purpose is to make sure the application is consistent with administration policy."

Numerous other officials suggested a more indirect type of coordination between their agencies and the governor's office. For example, the director of an education agency in the western United States said: "In deciding what we apply for we look at everything in terms of the 10-year early learning plan that we developed with the governor. We apply based on the fit, and every dollar we seek is meant to leverage some element within the action plan." An education official from the Midwest told a similar story, suggesting that in his agency "the commissioner does work closely with an education liaison from the governor's office, and I'm sure that helps the commissioner identify the priorities that drive our big applications."

Interestingly, the interviews suggested that coordination by the governor's office occurred not only for application-driven grants but also for those distributed by formula. In the case of the formulaic funds, the involvement by the governor's office seems to be focused on whether an agency should pursue the maximum amount of funding that a state is eligible to receive. An official from a southern health agency told a story of indirect influence on formulaic programming, suggesting that "the governor, through his overall policy and discussions with the commissioner, makes sure there's writing on the wall about something that is outside the direction he wants to go. The discretion is left up to the commissioner that the program, or more often an additional service within an existing program, is not going to be outside the governor's policy goals."

A federal liaison from a western state suggested a more active role for the governor. When asked if the governor's office is involved in trying to maximize formulaic funding, he replied, "Absolutely. For things we care about, we go through program by program and talk about the value—how they work separately, how they work together—for our priorities. We try to get them to give as close to the statutorily authorized amount as possible. If we can get $65 million, we push for $85 million."

An important part of the theoretical argument made earlier in this chapter is that governors have the ability to treat a portion of federal dollars as fungible and that they use that discretion strategically to pursue electoral ends. For obvious reasons, I did not ask the state-level informants I spoke with if the governor of their state (who more often than not appointed them) diverted grant funding away from targeted programs. I did, however, ask if the governor had influence over the ways in which grant monies were spent. Of course, in some ways this is just a more nuanced way of asking whether the governor can use grants to pursue policy goals, but the responses help to highlight the tools by which the executive influences the expenditure of federal funds and the zeal with which they use those tools.

When asked "How involved is the governor (or the governor's staff) in determining how . . . funds are spent?" interviewees consistently spoke of a significant level of involvement, particularly in the crafting of the budgets submitted with the grant applications. For example, the deputy head of a social services agency in a western state explained: "There is the Office of Financial Management in the governor's office, and we have a liaison there that we consult with. We usually don't have any trouble figuring out how to spend the money, but we do interface with them to be sure it is in line with what the governor's team thinks is reasonable."

A federal liaison from a different state spoke of a similar mechanism, suggesting: "Within the Office of Financial Management, the budget office plays a role in that. They are members of the governor's senior staff and have great relationships with the agency budget folks. They talk when developing the budget and figuring out where a grant might fill in, but also ask will the agency be able to spend the money and what should be done."

In some policy areas, such as transportation, higher education, and others, decisions about what projects should be emphasized, and ultimately how grant and own-source funds should be allocated within a particular spending category, are often made by commissions rather than individual agencies. Even in these cases, however, governors are likely to have significant influence because they are typically involved in the appointment of such commissions. A transportation official confirmed that neither his agency nor the legislature really "authorize the spending for the individual projects. We have the independent commission, who are appointed by the governor, and all spending decisions are devolved to them."

The comment of that official makes for a natural segue into the relative advantages that governors have over legislators in the strategic use of federal grant monies. The theory outlined here turns in large part on the assumption that governors are well positioned to use grants strategically and that legislatures, which may be controlled by another party or have different institutional incentives, cannot easily thwart such activities. The officials I interviewed consistently suggested that this was the case. For example, when asked if their agency coordinates with the legislature regarding grant applications and expenditure, they gave responses such as, "We don't specifically engage the legislature other than to inform the legislature" and "I go to the capital a lot to brief them on what we're doing, but we don't have to approach them to authorize spending for the individual projects." In explaining the legislature's lack of involvement in the process, one federal liaison said simply, "They tend to get caught up in their regular jobs." An official from a midwestern health agency suggested that "they look more programmatically. They don't go dollar by dollar through hundreds of millions in federal grants we get."

Despite the general advantage that informants described for governors in the fiscal federalism process, some did highlight specific conditions under which legislatures play a more active role in the pursuit and expenditure of federal monies. For example, the assistant director of a southern health agency explained:

> We can't spend a penny unless it is appropriated by the legislature. Some grants fall outside the normal fiscal year. If we receive an award during the budget cycle, we work with the department of finance and administration to have any matching or MOE requirement included in the Department's spending authority. If it's outside the normal cycle we are allowed to request an expansion of our spending authority. We have to send an expansion packet to the legislature and, in that case, we have to work pretty closely with them.

Two respondents indicated that recent fiscal stress had triggered increased engagement by legislators. Several relayed examples of singular issues that had caught the attention, and in some cases the ire, of legislators from their states. As an example of the latter, an official from an education agency in the Midwest suggested:

> It really depends on how much the legislature is paying attention. We could get a grant of $10 million for something that was politically unpopular, but if the legislature doesn't appropriate the money, then we can't spend any of it. A good example is the [redacted] proposal we put in a couple of years ago. Some members of the legislature expressed serious concerns because the proposal included a quality rating system for [redacted]. We lost some money, even though we did not get the grant, because that system was against the will of the legislature.

However, that official concluded by saying, "Still, even though they are both technically on equal footing, the governor has a real advantage when it comes to using grants politically."

Conclusion

This chapter offers a political theory of grant-related decision making in the states. That theory is grounded in the assumption that state actors have discretion in the pursuit and expenditure of federal funds, that state actors are constrained by cognitive and monetary resources in the number of grants they can pursue, and that governors have more power than other state-level actors over which grants a state pursues and the ways in which those monies are spent. This theory proposes that U.S. governors use federal grants-in-aid strategically in order to maximize electoral benefit for themselves and their parties and that they do so via two mechanisms. The first of these is "policy-seeking," whereby incumbents seek and spend grants in a way that allows them to deliver on promises made to core constituents. The second is "electoral opportunism," or the use of grants and grant-funded programming to sway noncore voters as elections approach. Rather than treating these mechanisms as independent of one another, the theory articulated here suggests that they may work in concert, with governors using grants for policy-seeking purposes early in their terms but becoming opportunists as elections approach. Finally, the theory proposes that, if we can uncover evidence of strategic use of grants-in-aid by U.S. governors, then we should also expect a relationship between grants and electoral success. More specifically, it offers the expectation that, all else being equal, higher grant totals will be associated with higher popularity and increased vote share for the incumbent's party.

Interviews conducted with gubernatorial staff, officials in executive agencies, and state legislators confirm many these theoretical assumptions and propositions. The assumption that states have some discretion in the pursuit and expenditure of federal funds is well established in previous research, but the assertion that governors are in a better position to take advantage of that discretion is not. Fortunately, informants regularly confirmed that governors wield significantly more power over grant-related decisions relative to other actors because of institutional capacity (e.g., Offices of Financial Management), control over executive agency and commission decision making (e.g., influence over appointments and strategic plans), and power over the budgetary agenda.

The proposition that governors would use grants strategically rather than simply chasing any and all federal monies is novel. However, all of the interviewees suggested that the governor of their state uses grants to pursue policy goals. The notion that this behavior is strategic is confirmed by the consistent references to coordination, both direct and indirect, between the governor's office and the executive agencies that form the primary interface with the fiscal federalism system. When speaking of what governors pursue through such coordination, the vast majority identified policies and goals that can be identified as characteristically Republican or Democratic, giving strong support to the partisan element of the theory. However, a few of those interviewed relayed stories suggesting that governors sometimes use grants to pursue policies other than those favored by core constituents, particularly as elections approach, which suggests that there is some electoral opportunism in grant-related decision making by governors.

Chapter Three

The Strategic Pursuit of Federal Grants

In 1999 then-candidate George W. Bush promised that his administration would "elevate abstinence education from an afterthought to an urgent goal." He delivered on that promise after moving into the Oval Office, increasing funding from $73 million a year in 2001 to $204 million in 2008. All in all, $1.5 billion in grant funding was delivered during his administration for "abstinence-only" education. The funding was available exclusively to programs teaching that abstinence is the only sure method for preventing pregnancy and sexually transmitted infections (STIs), that sex within the context of marriage is the standard for sexual activity, and that having sex outside the context of marriage will likely lead to psychological and physical harm.[1]

Not surprisingly, the program had numerous critics, from those suggesting that there was little or no scientific evidence validating the abstinence approach to those insisting that it willfully jeopardized the health and even the lives of teens.[2] One thing the vast majority of these critics had in common was that they were *not* members of the social conservative wing of the

Republican party, who remained (and remain) steadfast in their support of the program.[3]

By 2007, however, the din of criticism had reached a roar, and a number of governors began publicly refusing to apply for or accept Title V, Section 510 funding from the federal government. Some, like Ted Strickland of Ohio, suggested that his state was doing so because there was too little evidence of the policy's effectiveness.[4] However, a look at the states that refused funding suggests an additional motivation. All four of the states that first rejected the grant were headed by Democratic governors. By the end of President Bush's second term, 24 states had quit participating or announced their intention to do so, and most of those states were also headed by Democrats.

Another interesting part of this story comes from the states that refused abstinence-only funding while a Republican was governor. By the end of 2008, eight governors had "defected" from their party by refusing abstinence money. None of these publicly questioned the effectiveness of the program, but instead they blamed unpredictable federal allocations for their decision.' As a spokesperson for the governor of Idaho suggested, "The funding stream became inconsistent [and] we didn't know from one quarter to the next whether we'd be getting the rest of the money."[5] However, an examination of the politics in these states reveals a potential alternative motivation. The Republicans who eschewed the funds had a mean approval rating of 49% and were all facing reelection within two years. By contrast, the 13 Republican governors that continued to accept abstinence-only grants did not face the same electoral pressure or were much more popular, with an average approval rating of 59.5%.

The decision by governors to embrace or reject abstinence-only education is of interest to students of fiscal federalism for several reasons. First, as noted in the introductory chapter, it was in no way an isolated incident of grant-receipt decisions being made for seemingly political reasons. Second, the refusal of abstinence-only funding in some states is not well explained by existing theories of grant distribution. Those theories are divided primarily into two categories. "Supply-side" approaches emphasize federal preferences in the grant-in-aid system and suggest that shared party affiliations, strong challengers, status as a swing state or district, and loyalty to a winning presidential candidate all increase the amount of federal aid flowing into a jurisdiction.[6] Alternatively, "demand-side" approaches have explained the amount of aid that a state or locality receives primarily as a function of citizen appetite for a public good within a jurisdiction, the degree to which grants fulfill the basic needs of those same citizens, and the jurisdiction's capacity to produce the public goods in question.[7]

Unfortunately, neither of these approaches does a very good job of explaining the examples discussed above. In each case, federal preferences remained unchanged over time and so can offer no explanation for the change in funding patterns. Obviously, since these were gubernatorial decisions, a demand-side approach is more logical, but here the prevailing wisdom also fails to provide clarity. In Ohio, teen pregnancy rates were quite stable between 2006 when Governor Taft last applied for abstinence-only funding and 2007 when Governor Strickland announced that he would no longer do so. The state's fiscal condition also remained relatively constant during that period. Thus, changes in need and capacity do not offer much leverage in explaining the changes in the distribution of these grants. It is also hard to argue that shifting citizen preferences drove the decisions by governors. A Quinnipiac University Poll in late 2007 found that 40% of Ohioans opposed Governor Strickland's abandonment of abstinence-only sex education. That figure is statistically indistinguishable from the 36% of a sample surveyed in 2005–2006 that favored an exclusive focus on abstinence.[8]

While traditional approaches to grant distribution cannot explain recent decisions in the states, the political theory of state fiscal federalism decisions appears to do so quite well. It suggests that governors will typically seek and accept grant funding that helps them cater to core constituents but will be more open to grants that fund public goods desired by the median voter as elections approach or when approval is low. The theory also suggests that, since federal funding typically implies some growth in state expenditures, right-leaning governors whose core constituents favor smaller government will apply for and receive less grant money than their more liberal counterparts.

Several of the examples discussed above seem to validate these propositions. Abstinence-only education was (and remains) a policy strongly favored by the core constituency of the Republican Party. Republican governors were much more likely to continue accepting federal abstinence-only funding at the end of the Bush administration than were their Democratic counterparts. Among the limited number of Republicans that broke with the administration and rejected the grant, all were facing imminent reelection and were, on average, suffering from low approval ratings. Regardless of how well it fits, however, an anecdote cannot validate the utility or accuracy of a theory. For that reason, the remainder of this chapter provides systematic evidence that governors use federal grants-in-aid as a political resource—in other words, evidence that they apply for and receive funds that help them deliver policies to core constituents and/or woo noncore voters in times of electoral insecurity. The strategy for doing this is triangulation through the use of multiple data sources, dependent variables, and empirical methods.

The first set of analyses examines project- or application-driven grants-in-aid. These are programs for which a gubernatorial administration, or more specifically a bureaucratic agency within that administration, must apply in order to be considered for an award. These grants represent a smaller proportion of total federal aid relative to formulaic monies, but they afford governors a great many more choices in the potential programs they can fund. Moreover, the linkage between gubernatorial political preferences and grants (assuming one exists) is more direct. Here the analyses will move from general to specific. The first examines the proportion of the total number of discretionary grants received by governors that come from the Department of Health and Human Services (DHHS), a classic redistributive agency, versus the Department of Justice, which typically funds more conservative social regulatory policies. Specifically, this analysis looks for changes or consistency in these proportions in a sample of 12 states before, during, and after the 2006 gubernatorial elections. The second analysis of discretionary grants models the impact of partisan and electoral pressures on state receipt of federal funds across a sample of six project grants available to the states in recent decades.[9] Finally, the analysis examines applications to a single grant program through a brief case study of the Race to the Top competitive grant award offered by the Obama administration in 2009.

The second set of analyses tests for the impact of party preferences and electoral pressures on the receipt and use of waivers of federal requirements for the formulaic grant funding that states receive from the federal government. Because of the ways in which formulaic grants are distributed, governors are more constrained in their ability to alter the amount a state receives than in those in those programs that require an application. However, an important way that governors can influence the amount and character of aid flowing into their states through these programs is through waivers that allow states the discretion to structure service delivery or eligibility in a way that more

closely matches their preferences.[10] Because the ten largest formulaic programs represent roughly 80% of total federal assistance,[11] demonstrating that
partisanship, electoral security, or some combination of the two affects the
character of these programs through the use of waivers helps to confirm that
the politics of grants in the states have *substantive* import. Specifically, this
chapter examines work and time-limit waivers for Aid to Families with Dependent Children (AFDC) between 1992 and 1996, and 1915(c) Home Health
Care waivers to the Medicaid Program between 1998 and 2005.

Project Grants

Unlike in formulaic grants, state-level discretion is quite high when it
comes to project grants. Remember that these are funds for which gubernatorial administrations and the administrative agencies that work for them must
apply before a state can become an eligible recipient. As has been noted,
these types of grants do not represent as large a share of total federal monies
as formulaic grants, but they do offer states a remarkable menu of public programs from which to choose. The Catalogue of Federal Domestic Assistance
suggests that between 1993 and 2009 there were 849 project or cooperative
agreement grants that were both nationally focused (rather than targeted
at specific regions or places) and available to eligible state governments for
funding.[12]

The bulk of these programs are designed to appeal to as many potential
applicants as possible. The intuition behind this design is simple. The federal
government pursues its policy goals through the grant-in-aid system, and the
more states that apply for and receive a grant, the more successful is that
pursuit (in theory at least) in a particular area. On the other hand, the vast
majority of federal programs can also be classified as primarily distributive,
redistributive, regulatory, or social regulatory in nature. In other words, they
will help fund programs that (1) distribute benefits widely to a state's citizenry; (2) distribute benefits narrowly to a small, often low-income or otherwise vulnerable, set of citizens; (3) restrict private sector activity in order to
prevent fraud, environmental degradation, and so forth; or (4) restrict individual behavior that violates social or legal norms. An application to one
of these programs typically implies the expenditure of own-source funds on
the targeted good or service and, in the zero-sum environment of state budgets, that means the money cannot be spent on another public or private

good. As such, applying for and receiving a discretionary grant is an expression of policy preference that is closely analogous to the choice to spend more on some goods—say prison construction—than on others—say higher education.

Because of the need to apply for discretionary grants and the wide variety of preferences that those grants represent, they are a perfect place to test the political theory of state-level grant behavior outlined in chapter 2. Of course, the sheer volume of discretionary grants also makes them difficult to analyze. Because of the large number of grants that a governor might apply for and receive, it is a challenge to gain a representative picture of the ways they use these grants as a political resource. In order to address that challenge, it is best to use multiple data sources and multiple levels of analysis in search of consistent evidence of partisan and electoral motivations for grant receipt.

Project Grant Distributions from Two Agencies

The first step in this approach is to assess the degree to which a higher or lower percentage of the total discretionary grant *programs* that governors participate in come from different agencies. The intuition behind this approach is relatively straightforward. Because of the fiscal constraints discussed above as well as the administrative costs of applying for individual awards, there are a finite number of grant programs in which any gubernatorial administration can participate. If governors are using these applications to pursue political ends, then the distribution of grants they apply for should reflect the preferences of core constituents in good times and move back toward the median voter when electoral security is low.

As a proxy for the type of grants that governors might apply for, this section uses the federal agency that administers the program. More specifically, it examines the proportion of the total number of discretionary programs in which a state participates that originate in the Department of Health and Human Services (DHHS) and the Department of Justice (DOJ). In these cases, the agency serves as a good proxy for grant type because each agency in question administers grants that fit primarily into one policy type. For example, in 2010 DHHS offered 149 project grants for which state governments were eligible to apply. More than 71% of those were clearly redistributive in nature, taking tax dollars gathered from the population and targeting them at a narrow subgroup of citizens. A small sample of exemplar programs includes Human Immunodeficiency Virus (HIV) / Acquired Immunodeficiency Virus

Syndrome (AIDS) Surveillance (93.944), Healthy Start Initiative (93.926), Mentoring Children of Prisoners (93.616), Minority Health and Health Disparities Research (93.307), Clinical Research Loan Repayment Program for Individuals from Disadvantaged Backgrounds (93.220), and Family Planning Services (93.217). The percentage coded as redistributive would be even higher, but it does not include programs targeted at narrow groups that are typically positively constructed, such as the aged and those with chronic diseases (other than HIV/AIDS).

The mission of the Department of Justice is equally easy to divine based on the grants it awards. In 2010, the DOJ offered 39 project grants for which states were eligible to apply. More than 69% of these were social regulatory in nature, meaning that they were designed to help state and local governments catch and punish citizens that violate society's laws, prevent such violations from occurring, or compensate the victims of such violations. For example, in that year the agency offered the Edward Byrne Memorial State and Local Law Enforcement Assistance Discretionary Grants Program (16.580), Economic, High-Tech, and Cyber Crime Prevention grants (16.752), and the Capital Case Litigation program (16.746). Again, the percentage coded as social regulatory could easily be higher, but I do not include programs designed to reduce the exposure of children to criminal activity such as the Gangs Resistance Education and Training program (16.737). Additionally, DOJ programs that contain a distributive element, such as the Criminal Justice Research and Development Graduate Research Fellowships (16.562), are not counted as social regulatory even though they obviously address that policy type in some fashion.

Based on the types of grants that these agencies administer, the political theory of state-level fiscal federalism suggests that Republican governors should apply for more grants from the DOJ, while Democrats should preference the programs awarded by DHHS. When electoral security is low, the theory suggests that these patterns may reverse themselves. In order to test these expectations, I focus on a random sample of 12 of the 36 states that held gubernatorial elections in 2006. My empirical strategy is to compare the percentage of total discretionary grants received by the state that came from DHHS and DOJ (1) two years before that election, (2) in the election year, and (3) two years after the election. This allows for variation in the party and in some cases the person of the governor, while holding the state constant.

The 2006 election was chosen because it represents a "typical" cycle where the majority of governorships are up for grabs and because it was the last such election before the American Recovery and Reinvestment Act of 2009, which significantly increased the number of grants awarded by many federal agencies. The sample includes Alabama, Arkansas, Colorado, Connecticut, Illinois, Kansas, Massachusetts, Maryland, New York, Ohio, Pennsylvania, and Tennessee. Eight of the states were controlled by Republicans before the election, while four were headed by Democrats. Seven governors from the sample ran for reelection, three were term-limited out of office, and two retired. Of the states where the incumbent ran, six held their seats, but the governor's office changed parties in all five of the states where races were open.

The results from the comparisons of grant receipt in these 12 states provide considerable support for the assertion that gubernatorial partisanship influences the types of grant programs that states participate in. Those results are presented in table 3.1. For each state, the table describes what transpired during the election of 2006 (column 2) along with the grant percentages from DOJ and DHHS in 2004 (column 3), 2006 (column 4), and 2008 (column 5). In 100% of the cases where a different political party held the governorship in 2008 compared with 2004, the grant percentages behaved as expected. Democratic victories were responsible for all such instances in this sample, and in each case the percentage of a state's discretionary grants from the DOJ went down, while the percentage from the DHHS went up. This suggests that Democratic governors increased their focus on securing redistributive grants rather than social regulatory grants relative to their Republican predecessors. This, of course, is in line with the expected preferences of the core Democratic constituents that put them in office.

In cases where there was no change in party, the expectation was that there should be no significant change in grant percentages. The results fully support this expectation in two-thirds of those instances. In one case—Kansas—the results are partially supportive because DHHS grants remained unchanged, but DOJ grants went down unexpectedly. Thus, the result is generally supportive of the argument that incumbent governors will stick with the preferences of co-partisans that kept them in office. For Republicans, this meant a consistent focus on the social regulatory funding preferred by their base, while for Democrats it meant more redistributive grants from DHHS.

Interestingly, the findings provide almost no support for the expectation

Table 3.1   Comparing state participation in project grants from two agencies,
2004–2008

State	What happens in 2006	DOJ and DHHS grant percentages by year		
		2004	2006	2008
Alabama	R seeks and wins reelection	5.5; 34	6.3; 31	5.2; 34
Arkansas	R term-limited, D takes over	7; 33.1	9.6; 28	5.1; 35.7
Colorado	R does not seek reelection, D takes over	10; 34	8.3; 31.2	5.6; 36.6
Connecticut	R seeks and wins reelection	6.4; 35.6	7.5; 30.4	5.1; 37.4
Illinois	D seeks and wins reelection	4.9; 36	7.2; 28.9	4.4; 34.2
Kansas	D seeks and wins reelection	7.8; 33.7	10.9; 23	4.8; 32.5
Maryland	R seeks reelection, D takes over	8.1; 34.6	9.1; 28.3	4.2; 37
Massachusetts	R does not seek reelection, D takes over	7.9; 33	7.8; 28	4.5; 35.1
New York	R does not seek reelection, D takes over	8.8; 33.7	10; 27	6.3; 36
Ohio	R does not seek reelection, D takes over	7.8; 34.8	8.5; 29.3	4.5; 36.5
Pennsylvania	D seeks and wins reelection	7.8; 35.5	8.7; 29.4	7.6; 35.3
Tennessee	D seeks and wins reelection	8.9; 35.7	8.6; 27.5	7.8; 34.9

that electoral pressures will change the types of discretionary grants that governors receive. Based on the theory articulated here, I expected grant proportions to move *within* states based on whether the focus was on 2004 and 2008, which were nonelection years for all these governors, or 2006, when most of them were running for reelection. What the analyses reveals, however, is somewhat different. In almost all cases, regardless of whether the governor was a Democrat or a Republican, running for reelection or not, or popular versus unpopular in 2006, grants from the DOJ went up, while those from DHHS went down. This result is not the product of a change in the number of available grants from DOJ and DHHS, which remained relatively constant across the period. It may simply reflect the fact that "tough on crime" rhetoric and programs are a favorite and persistent campaign platform for politicians from both parties. Whatever the explanation, the result does not support the expectation that Republican governors would adjust their grant profile toward DHHS programs during the election year to appeal to noncore moderate voters.

Funds Received from Specific Project Grants

This section turns from the receipt of different categories of grants in and around one election cycle to an analysis of specific project grant awards to the American states between 1993 and 2005. Again, because of the large number of project grants available during that time period, drawing reliable conclusions about the behavior of the "average" state is challenging. For example, a "representative" sample of the project grants for which states could have applied during the past couple of decades would need to include 473 programs. As an alternative, this section draws a purposive sample of six policies that vary on major dimensions *except for* the need to apply for funding. By examining programs administered by different agencies, some of which appeal to Democratic and some to Republican constituencies, some with matching requirements and some without, some with maintenance of effort restrictions and some without, the analysis can approximate a least-similar systems design. In other words, the selection of cases that share very few similarities helps to control for alternative explanations for observed relationships. If, despite all these differences, partisan and electoral variables predict application decisions in a manner that is consistent with theoretical expectations, then we can have greater confidence that these factors truly do influence state-level decisions about which grants to pursue in the larger population of federal awards.

The six grant programs analyzed here are:

- *The Edward Byrne Memorial State and Local Law Enforcement Assistance Discretionary Grants Program.* The program is administered by the Office of Justice Assistance (OJA) within the Department of Justice and is intended to improve "law enforcement programs; prosecution and court programs; prevention and education programs; corrections and community corrections programs; drug treatment and enforcement programs; planning, evaluation, and technology improvement programs; and crime victim and witness programs." There is no matching requirement, but the OJA explicitly states that Byrne funds are not to be used to supplant state or local funds.
- *The Plant and Animal Disease, Pest Control, and Animal Care Program* administered by the Animal and Plant Health Inspection Service within the Department of Agriculture. The grant is designed to

"protect U.S. agriculture from economically injurious plant and animal diseases and pests, ensure the safety and potency of veterinary biologic, and ensure the humane treatment of animals." It has no matching or maintenance of effort requirement, but it does require a cost-sharing arrangement between the federal government and the recipient jurisdiction.

- *The Manufacturing Extension Partnership* (MEP) administered by the National Institute of Standards and Technology within the Department of Commerce in order "to establish, maintain, and support manufacturing extension centers and services . . . and partner with the States in developing such technical assistance programs and services for their manufacturing base." The program has a graduated matching requirement. For the first three years, recipients must provide at least 50% of the funds required to create and maintain the center. In the fourth year that climbs to 60%, and then to 66.7% for year five and beyond.

- *The Air Pollution Control Program Support Grant* administered by the Office of Air and Radiation with the Environmental Protection Agency. These grants are designed to "assist . . . in planning, developing, establishing, improving, and maintaining adequate programs for the continuing prevention and control of air pollution and/or in the implementation of national primary and secondary air quality standards" as well as address issues of environmental justice. This is a matching grant where programs may receive up to 60% federal funding for total program costs. Awardees must contribute not only a minimum of 40%, but also meet a maintenance of effort requirement.

- *The Public Health and Social Services Emergency Fund* administered by the DHHS. The fund was created to "provide supplemental funding for public health and social service emergencies." It has no matching, maintenance of effort, or cost-sharing requirement.

- *Family Planning Grants* administered by the Office of Population Control within DHHS. The program is designed to "provide educational, counseling, comprehensive medical and social services necessary to enable individuals to freely determine the number and spacing of their children." The program has no matching or maintenance of effort requirements.

All of these programs distributed more than $80 million to the states in the last year for which data is available. Because of that size, they offer incumbents the opportunity to provide tangible benefits to constituents and, as such, the potential incentive to manipulate receipt for political purposes. The first three focus on social regulation or economic development and should be favored, all else being equal, by the core constituents of Republican governors. Alternatively, the latter three focus on the regulation of industry, the provision of social welfare services, or reproductive freedom and should therefore be more appealing to Democratic constituencies.

The dependent variables in subsequent analyses are the per capita inflation adjusted amount received from each of these programs in each state and year. The series are not integrated and thus do not need to be differenced. The models discussed below include a correction for first-order autocorrelation and state fixed effects, which ensure that coefficients represent relationships *within* rather than *across* states. The key independent variables include an indicator of a Republican governor and interactions that separately capture Republicans and Democrats running for reelection in a given year. The excluded category in this specification is Democratic governors in nonelection years. The control variables include demand-side factors such as unemployment, per capita income, total expenditures, urbanization, indicators of unified Democratic control of the legislature and unified control of the legislature and the statehouse, the measure of citizen ideology, and Beyle's index of formal gubernatorial powers. In addition to these variables, the models contain controls designed to capture "supply-side" arguments that project grant distribution is in part a function of national politics. These include indicators of presidential election year and shared partisanship between the White House and a governor's mansion. The results do not change substantially when the sample is restricted to allow for the inclusion of gubernatorial approval, which is not available in every state and year, so those models are not presented or discussed at length in this section.

The results from the analyses of these six programs are presented in table 3.2. They are quite supportive of the expectation that incumbents favor grants for programs preferred by their core constituents. In the case of the Byrne Law Enforcement Assistance, the Plant and Animal Disease Control, and the Manufacturing Extension Partnership programs—all social regulatory or distributive programs—the state received significantly larger amounts of funding when headed by a Republican not running for reelection than a

Table 3.2 State-level awards across six project grants, 1993–2005

Independent variables	Grants					
	Byrne	Disease and pest	MEP	Air pollution	Public health and social services	Family planning
Republican, no election	0.282*	0.228*	0.313**	−0.081*	0.036	−0.097**
	(0.171)	(0.125)	(0.122)	(0.045)	(0.077)	(0.038)
Republican election	−0.408*	−0.337*	−0.062	−0.050	0.106*	0.015
	(0.215)	(0.232)	(0.171)	(0.063)	(0.060)	(0.020)
Democratic election	−0.112	−0.102	−0.17	0.009	0.123	−0.036
	(0.268)	(0.261)	(0.214)	(0.080)	(0.166)	(0.049)
Total expenditure	0.264**	0.102	0.357***	0.007	0.241***	0.017
	(0.095)	(0.081)	(0.064)	(0.024)	(0.066)	(0.024)
Unemployment	−0.092	−0.285	0.088	−0.012	0.074	−0.029
	(0.122)	(0.193)	(0.059)	(0.022)	(0.075)	(0.020)
Personal income	3.7e-05	4.1e-05*	−1.1e-05	−2e-05**	8e-05***	2.1e-05**
	(2.4e-05)	(2.2e-05)	(1.6e-05)	(5.9e-06)	(2.1e-05)	(8.3e-06)
Urbanization	0.139*	0.003	0.074	0.010	−0.002	−0.009
	(0.082)	(0.072)	(0.051)	(0.019)	(0.030)	(0.025)

Citizen ideology	-0.006	-0.003	-0.006	-0.011**	0.011	0.001
	(0.013)	(0.018)	(0.009)	(0.003)	(0.009)	(0.002)
Dem. legislature	0.075	0.214	-0.030	0.021	0.035	0.012
	(0.107)	(0.212)	(0.069)	(0.026)	(0.034)	(0.026)
Unified government	0.119	0.077	0.106	-0.025	-0.044	-0.043
	(0.171)	(0.200)	(0.117)	(0.043)	(0.057)	(0.038)
Governor's power	0.301	0.072	0.214	-0.046	0.113	0.039
	(0.443)	(0.320)	(0.278)	(0.104)	(0.138)	(0.100)
Presidential election	-0.098	-0.144	-0.081	-0.021	0.241***	-0.002
	(0.122)	(0.169)	(0.098)	(0.036)	(0.062)	(0.015)
Same party as president	-0.340**	0.069	-0.031	-0.021	-0.069	0.055
	(0.142)	(0.234)	(0.097)	(0.036)	(0.096)	(0.050)
Intercept	-11.809	-0.694	-7.257	0.873	-4.056	0.211
	(4.849)	(5.202)	(3.705)	(1.389)	(2.191)	(1.843)
State FE significant?	yes	yes	yes	yes	yes	yes
$N =$	539	539	539	539	539	539
$R^2 =$	0.09	0.05	0.09	0.1	0.3	0.17
F (prob>F) =	3.39 (.0001)	3.01 (.0027)	3.74 (.0000)	3.90 (.0000)	103.6 (.0000)	1.94 (.05)

Note: Numbers in parentheses are standard errors. * $p<.1$, ** $p<.05$, *** $p<.01$

Democrat with the same electoral security. In addition to being consistent with the theory, the effects of gubernatorial partisanship are substantively meaningful, suggesting that a change to a Republican governor was associated with an average increase of about .2-standard deviation in aid from these three grants. That effect was comparable with the impact of other significant predictors, including the total amount that a state spends.

Also consistent with expectations was the finding that states received more money from the Air Pollution Control Program Support and Family Planning grants when headed by Democrats who were not facing an electoral constraint. Here the effects were even larger, with gubernatorial partisanship associated with an average .25-standard deviation change in the amount of grant aid flowing into the state. Only in the model of Public Health and Social Services Emergency funding was there no significant difference in fund receipt between governors from different parties not seeking reelection.

The models also provide some support, though it is more mixed, for the expectation that incumbent governors will begin to pursue grants preferred by noncore constituents as elections approach. States headed by Republicans did receive *less* funding from the Byrne and Plant Disease programs when running for reelection compared with those headed by Democratic governors in the same state not facing an electoral constraint, which is consistent with the theoretical prediction that incumbents will move toward programs favored by noncore constituents in election years. Also consistent with the theory, Republicans running for reelection received more funding from the Public Health Emergency fund than their Democratic counterparts not running. In the case of pest control and public health grants, these electoral effects were quite large.

In three of the six cases examined here, the interactions between party and election failed to reach statistical significance, however, suggesting that incumbents did not moderate their grant-seeking behavior when facing an election. Thus, it is difficult to say that these results strongly support the electoral story. It is possible to say with caution, however, that there are probably some electoral influences on grant receipt by governors. In five of the six models the indicator of Republicans seeking reelection is in the right direction, even if the coefficients fail to reach statistical significance, and we would likely not see this type of consistency if the relationship between electoral security and grant seeking were completely stochastic. As noted above, this result did not change when controlling for gubernatorial approval in the limited set of states where that variable is consistently available.

Though they support the expectation that governors use grants as a political resource, at least in the case of the partisan theory of grant-seeking behavior, one obvious challenge to these results is that they model grant *receipt* rather than grant *applications*. However, it is important to remember that the models include numerous controls for the amount of grants received as well as the estimation of state fixed effects, which ensure that partisan comparisons are made only *within* each state. With these factors in mind, it is difficult to imagine that the observed relationship between party and grant receipt is completely independent of grant application decisions by governors. For that to be the case there would need to be some unobserved factor that varies within states and causes each party to be more successful at securing the grants their constituents prefer and less successful at getting those preferred by the other party, despite the fact that they are applying with the same frequency to these different kinds of grants. The probability of such a variable existing may not be 0, but it is likely relatively small. Additionally, these results regarding grant receipt accord well with recently published work that does examine grant applications explicitly.[13]

Applications to the Race to the Top Competition

The results discussed above suggest that partisan and electoral factors influence grant receipt in the states. This section provides a more in-depth exploration of the impact of gubernatorial party and impending election on grant application decisions. More specifically, it examines applications to the Race to the Top (RTTT) competition announced on July 24, 2009, by President Barack Obama.

With over $4.35 billion of promised funds for its first two phases, Race to the Top represented the largest competitive federal grant in the history of U.S. education. Each state, along with the District of Columbia, was invited by the Department of Education to submit an application. This process was divided into two stages. States that chose to do so could apply to Phase 1 by January 19, 2010, and states that chose not to apply for Phase 1 or did not get applications competed by the deadline, as well as those who applied but did not receive funding, could submit an application for Phase 2 by June 1, 2010. Ultimately, 12 applicants to the first two phases received funding: Delaware,

Tennessee, Florida, Georgia, Hawaii, Maryland, Massachusetts, New York, North Carolina, Ohio, Rhode Island, and Washington, D.C.

Each state that applied was awarded points in six (primary) categories, with a total of 500 points possible. These included state success factors, standards and assessments, data systems that support instruction, great teachers and leaders, turning around the lowest achieving schools, and a general category. Some of these, like points awarded for components of a state data system, were largely formulaic. In other words, if you put a data system in place, you received the points. Others, like those awarded for strategies to turn around failing schools, were discretionary based on assessments of feasibility and probability of success made by education experts. In order to gather these experts, the Department of Education put out a nationwide call, ultimately receiving 1,500 nominations. From these they selected 58 reviewers who scored the applications submitted by states.

The RTTT competition is a good place to test for partisan and electoral influences on grant applications outlined above for a variety of reasons. The first is its size. The proposed awards were big enough to allow incumbents to make a meaningful promise of increased spending on education. Indeed, the winners in the first round of the competition received an award equivalent to roughly 7% of their total K–12 expenditures in the previous year.

The RTTT is also a good place to test the political model of state grant decision making because of the application cost and process. The Department of Education estimated that it would take approximately 642 hours for a state to put together the RTTT application, which had a length of approximately 1,000 pages. Thus, it was far from a costless activity for governors and their departments of education, who were primarily responsible for spearheading the application process. The process also speaks to the validity of RTTT as a test. Awards were made based on the judgment of a panel of education experts rather than by national politicians. This allows the analysis to partially control for the electoral ambitions of national actors, which can have a significant influence on the distribution of aid.

Finally, because of the variation among applicants, RTTT is a good place to test a model of the partisan and electoral motivation for grant applications. Despite the fact that the competition took place in the context of the Great Recession of 2008–9, which compelled almost 70% of states to *reduce* spending on K–12 education, not every state chose to apply and only 29 states took full advantage of the opportunity to submit two applications. The dependent variable in subsequent analyses captures this variation or, more specifically, the number of applications that a state filed in Phase I and Phase II of the first round of RTTT.

Typically, education policy has been identified as something that both Democrats and Republicans support, but there were some unique features of the reform agenda that undergirded the RTTT competition. On the Republican side, Governor Rick Perry of Texas made headlines by challenging the competition as an unwelcome federal intrusion into state and local prerogatives. He suggested that states "must not surrender control to the federal bureaucracy" and that by creating the competition the Obama administration had "put a target on the backs of Texas leaders, taxpayers, and employers."[14] Ultimately, Texas chose not to file an application to either phase of the first round. Moreover, Governor Perry's argument seems to have resonated with Republican voters. At the very least, it is safe to conclude that the party elite *believed* that it did. All four of the strongest candidates in the 2012 Republican presidential primary battle—Mitt Romney, Rick Santorum, Newt Gingrich, and Ron Paul—took public positions against the competition.[15]

Interestingly, key members of the Democratic core constituency, namely, teachers' unions, were also opposed to the RTTT's agenda. More than 25% (138 of 500) of the points available in the application were awarded for laws and contract schemes that threatened or abolished seniority-based compensation and permanent job security. For example, high-scoring applications needed to demonstrate that budget-forced teacher layoffs would be based on the quality of the teacher, not simply on seniority, which was contrary to the practice in 15 states that operated under explicit "last in / first out" systems. Another 40 of the 500 points were most available to "charter-friendly" states. For these and other reasons, major teachers' unions around the nation opposed, sometimes vehemently, the Race to the Top program.[16] The president of the New York State Union of Teachers, a union associated with the American Federation of Teachers and the National Education Association, summarized the opposition to the program, claiming, "We've gone from no child left behind to every child—except the ones that win—left behind."[17]

Union opposition made RTTT more challenging for Democrats. As Deputy Education Commissioner of New York John King explained, the application process was "difficult and frustrating" due to the need to navigate "all of the competing interests in New York" and "all of the limits we had with the laws and collective-bargaining agreements in place and the political reality of the Legislature," which is strongly allied with teachers' unions.[18] Despite these challenges, New York filed applications in both of the initial phases of the competition.

The New York case is a good reminder that, while union opposition was strong, Race to the Top was one of the major early policy initiatives of a very popular Democratic president. Additionally, teachers' unions may be a powerful interest group, but they are far from the only members of the Democratic core constituency. And indeed, union opposition did not keep major Democratic organizations such as the Democratic Governors' Association and Democrats for Education Reform from supporting RTTT during and after the competition.

Given the factors described above, it is reasonable to expect that multiple applications to the RTTT competition would be more desirable to Democratic core constituents than to those of the Republican Party. The political theory of grant decision making suggests, therefore, that Republican incumbents not running for reelection in 2010 should have been less aggressive in the pursuit of RTTT funds. Alternatively, it expects that Republicans facing an election in that year would have been more likely to file multiple applications. The independent variables capturing gubernatorial party and its interaction with election year are the same as in previous models.

The model also includes a host of variables that control for state-level need and demand for RTTT funds as well as the capacity to produce high-quality education. I simultaneously measure the need for high-quality education and a state's capacity to produce it with the National Assessment of Educational Progress (NAEP) scores. Due to the limited degrees of freedom in a single-year analysis, I combine 4th and 8th grade math and reading proficiency in a single indicator of average proficiency within a state. The model also includes a measure of the proportion of total 2008 education spending within a state made up by federal dollars. Since the bulk of the numerator is composed of Title I funds, which are received disproportionately by poorer states, this variable primarily captures fiscal need. However, because the remainder of the numerator is made up of other grants from the U.S. Department of Education, it also reflects the prior success of the state in securing non-formulaic federal education funding.

I capture the "demand" for education within each state by measuring the payoff that governors expect to receive from educational improvements. Specifically, models include a measure of the number of times they claim credit for making such improvements in their State of the State Addresses. This measure assumes that, as politicians with an electoral motivation, they will spend more time talking about educational reform in states where citizens have greater demand for that good. The measure is created via content analysis of 2008 speeches, looking for any mention of government action relating to providing education goods and/or services for the purpose of bettering the citizens of the state.[19] Claims were only coded if the good or service had already been provided by the state as opposed to a promise of future action. For example, Alabama Governor Don Siegelman's statement, "Today, Alabama is engaged in the single largest school construction project in our history. . . . That has been done, and we did it together," was coded as one claim (State line.org).[20] The measure ranges between 0 and 8, with a mean of 2.34 claims in the average state.

The model discussed below captures interest group influence—another type of demand—with two proxies. First, it measures union influence with the donations (weighted by population) in 2008 to state-level candidates by the National Education Association and its affiliates. Campaign contributions provide the most direct (available) measure of the electoral power of these organizations and the potential power they may have influenced over politicians considering an RTTT application. These data were gathered from the National Institute on Money in State Politics, a nonpartisan watchdog group that tracks campaign donations to state-level candidates.[21] Second, it captures the power of groups committed to the creation and maintenance of charter schools. Specifically, the model includes the grade assigned to each state for its charter school policies by the Center for Education Research (CER) in 2006.[22] Finally, the model is conditional on whether the state won in the first round of the competition and on whether the governor was being term-limited out of office in 2010.

The results from the model are presented in table 3.3. Because the dependent variable takes on three ranked values, it is estimated as an ordered probit regression with robust standard errors. The control variables perform largely as expected. States that already had relatively lenient charter policies and those in which the governor expected a larger payoff from educational reform were more likely to submit multiple applications. On the other hand, states where students were already performing at a higher level and those that won in the first round were significantly less likely to do so.

The findings are also very supportive of partisan expectations about grant

Table 3.3   Applications to rounds I and II of the
Race to the Top competition

Variables	Coefficients
Republican, no election	−2.717***
	(0.743)
Republican election	1.792**
	(0.641)
Democrat election	0.184
	(0.489)
NAEP scores	−0.071*
	(0.032)
Federal/state spending ratio	6.328
	(0.510)
Education credit claiming	0.285**
	(0.105)
NEA contributions	−0.907
	(0.663)
Charter score	0.515**
	(0.175)
Won in round I	−3.514***
	(0.581)
Term-limited	−0.402
	(0.936)
$N =$	50
Pseudo $R^2 =$	0.35
Wald (prob>chi^2) =	130.27(.0000)

Note: Numbers in parentheses are standard errors. *p<.05,
**p<.01, ***p<.001

applications as well as those that expect opportunistic grant-seeking behavior from incumbents as elections approach. Substantively, they suggest that Republican governors who were not seeking reelection in 2010 had a .35 lower probability of filing multiple applications than did Democrats who were also free from the electoral constraint. Substantively, this represents a larger impact than any other significant predictor except having won in the first round.[23] Alternatively, the significant and positive coefficient on the interaction term for Republican governors in an election year indicates that the pattern was different for this group. Specifically, the coefficient suggests that Republican incumbents seeking reelection in 2010 had a .26 *higher* likelihood of filing multiple RTTT applications.

Formulaic Grants and Waivers

The preceding section provides clear evidence that governors pursue project and cooperative agreement grants-in-aid strategically. The results consistently suggest that these funds are sought in order to provide goods desired by co-partisans. They also indicate, though less consistently, that governors apply for grants that appeal to those outside their core constituency when electoral security is low. Application-driven grants represented over $120 billion spread across almost 1,000 programs in fiscal year 2011. As such, they are a substantively important vehicle for analyzing the ways in which governors can use fiscal federalism for political and electoral ends.

As noted above, however, over 80% of federal grants made to state and local governments are distributed by formula rather than application. The Medicaid program alone represents more than twice as much spending as all project and cooperative agreement grants combined. So while the latter are a legitimate place to test the theory outlined in this project, finding evidence that governors also strategically manipulate grant receipt in the much larger formulaic programs would increase the substantive importance of a state-focused political theory of fiscal federalism. Testing for relationships between partisan or electoral goals and formulaic grants also offers a more stringent test of one of the theory's major propositions. This is because the discretion that governors enjoy in determining the receipt of funds allocated by established statutory formula is considerably lower, and the cost for manipulating those funds is considerably higher, than it is for grants that require an application.

With that said, there are numerous ways in which governors can influence the amount of formulaic funding flowing into their states. These are huge programs with complex award criteria, which means that the exact allocation of federal dollars that a state can receive in any given year may not be precisely determined. In fact, there are numerous examples of what might be thought of as "wiggle room" where even formulaic allocations become somewhat negotiable. Examples are the use of "good cause" exceptions by state agencies as a tool to maintain federal Temporary Assistance to Needy Families (TANF) allocations; state activities such as the development of "Energy Assurance Plans" designed to create eligibility for formulaic funds distributed by programs like the American Recovery and Reinvestment Act of 2009 (ARRA); or funds distributed formulaically by DOI for habitat protection where the allocation depends in large part on the identification of qualifying land by state agencies. Members of gubernatorial administrations interviewed for this project suggested that there is significant variation in the aggressiveness with which governors pursue these dollars. Governors can also influence the flow of formulaic monies through numerous other means such as power over the provision of optional services in the case of Medicaid or over commissions responsible for project selection in the case of Highway Trust Funds allocations.

Scholars have also identified another powerful tool that governors use to influence even formulaically funded federal programs within their borders, arguing that much of the "action" in U.S. federalism now occurs in negotiations between national and subnational executives. This idea of executive federalism suggests that the scope and character of federal programs implemented in the states is increasingly determined, not by eligibility and benefit decisions made by state legislatures, but rather by the implementation discretion exercised by governors.[24] This discretion most often comes in the form of demonstration or programmatic waivers granted by federal agencies in numerous policy areas, including education, welfare, environmental protection, transportation, and, most consequentially, health.

Generally speaking, waivers are an exemption from certain requirements contained in federal programs. Technically, they are a delegation of authority by Congress to the executive branch that allows it to grant implementing jurisdictions discretion to deviate (in a circumscribed manner) from federal law. As such, the authority for waivers can be found in congressional statute. For example, in the case of Medicaid—the largest program in which waivers are frequently granted—Section 1115 of the Social Security Act (SSA) gives the executive relatively broad freedom to experiment with different types of service delivery at the state level. Section 1915 of the SSA gives it discretion to design more specific alternative programs, like those targeted at clients who would benefit from home- or community-based service provision.

Research on the use of waivers suggests that they allow states to have a very meaningful effect on the character of federal programming within their states. In the case of welfare policy, studies demonstrate that numerous states were able to use waivers to transform direct assistance administered under AFDC into "workfare" programs years before the passage of the TANF act mandated work requirements and time limits for the receipt of aid. Not surprisingly, the results also suggest a political dimension to these transformations, with Republican governors who counted a larger number of fundamentalist Protestants among their core constituents being more likely to seek work-related waivers.[25] In the case of Medicaid waivers, research suggests that they have had a significant impact on the design of long-term care policies and the provision of health insurance to low-income children, and have occasionally fostered large-scale changes to low-income health care provision like the ones evident in Tennessee's TenCare system.[26] Scholars suggest that Medicaid waivers have been attractive to and sought by both liberal and conservative states, arguing that Democratic governors see waivers as a way to expand services, while Republicans tend to use increased discretion to more narrowly target Medicaid services at certain groups or geographic areas and to control costs.[27]

The political theory of fiscal federalism offered here suggests that governors will typically pursue grants that provide public goods desired by their core constituents, but that they may shift their focus to grants preferred by the median voter as elections approach. The remainder of this section tests whether these propositions hold when governors apply for and use discretion in the implementation of formulaically funded programs. I test propositions regarding waivers and formulaic grants to the states in analyses of Aid to Families with Dependent Children (AFDC) and Medicaid. These are ideal places to test for the strategic pursuit and use of discretionary waivers by governors because of the size of welfare and health care grant programs. They also offer opportunities to examine both the specific character of the waivers that governors apply for (in the case of AFDC) and the impact that those waivers have on the inflows of federal funding (in the case of Medicaid).

Aid to Families with Dependent Children

The first analysis focuses on the pursuit of waivers by U.S. governors to impose work requirements and time limits on welfare receipt *before* the passage of the Temporary Aid to Needy Families act codified those requirements in federal welfare policy. The federal government actually authorized waivers to Aid to Families with Dependent Children implementation requirements in 1962. However, very few states sought this discretion until after 1992, when George H. W. Bush made state experimentation with AFDC a major part of his welfare reform agenda.[28] He encouraged states to use waivers to experiment with eligibility standards, promote "responsibility" among recipients, and, most importantly for this analysis, to impose work requirements and benefit time limits. Upon election, President Clinton quickly accelerated the pursuit of waivers by eliminating cost neutrality provisions and creating a fast-track approval process. The resultant growth in the states' pursuit of these discretionary tools was remarkable. In 1992, five states had waivers to impose work requirements and ten had been granted the discretion to impose time limits. By 1996, the year TANF was signed into law, only 13 states did *not* have work requirement waivers, and the number imposing time limits had grown to 25.

Historically, Republican constituents prefer smaller welfare rolls and less-generous benefit payments. They have also been more likely to distinguish between "deserving" and "undeserving" recipients.[29] I expect, therefore, that in order to provide policy goods to those constituents, Republican governors were more likely to receive work requirement and time limit waivers for their AFDC programs. Of course, the theory offered here suggests that the use of the grants-in-aid system to deliver benefits to core constituents may be moderated by electoral insecurity when politicians have an incentive to use the system to cater to the median voter. We might, therefore, expect that the likelihood that Republican governors would pursue these waivers would decline in election years. It is hard to say, however, if that expectation will hold true in the case of welfare reform. Research shows that public support for both work requirements and time limits increased significantly during the period under study and that these reforms were supported by a majority of Americans by 1996.[30]

To test expectations regarding the strategic application for AFDC implementation discretion by U.S. governors, I analyze work requirement and time limit waivers between 1992 and 1996. Specifically, I create a count measure coded 0 if a state had neither, 1 if it either, and 2 if it had both in a given year. The key independent variables include the party of the governor (1 = Republican), an indicator of election year, and the interaction of these variables.[31] The model also contains controls for alternative explanations for AFDC waivers, including AFDC expenditures as a proportion of total expenditures, AFDC recipients as a proportion of total population, percentage of state residents living in poverty, state wealth (measured as income per capita), state tax effort,[32] a measure of citizen ideology,[33] the Beyle measure of the governor's formal powers,[34] and an indicator of unified government. In order to account for the fact that public opinion regarding work requirements and time limits was changing during the period under study, the model also contains year fixed effects.[35] Because the dependent variable is a count that does not suffer from excessive zeros or over-dispersion, I estimate a Poisson regression with robust standard errors.

The model of AFDC waivers is presented in table 3.4, and the results provide considerable evidence that governors strategically pursue discretion in the implementation of formulaically funded programs. The coefficient on the indicator of gubernatorial partisanship is positive and significant, suggesting that the work requirement and time limit waivers were more likely to be received by states with Republican governors. Because of the inclusion of the interaction term, the partisanship variable represents the impact of having a Republican governor in a nonelection year. The interaction between partisanship and election is negative and significant, however, indicating that the likelihood of state with a Republican governor having one or both of these types of waivers decreases in election years. Substantively, the interaction suggests that the expected number of waivers goes up by .25, or approximately .33-standard deviations, when a state has a Republican governor not running for reelection rather than a Democratic governor. It also shows, however, that the differences between the parties disappear if the Republican is seeking reelection. So the analysis of AFDC waivers suggests that governors do pursue discretion in the implementation of formulaically funded programs in a way that matches the preferences of core constituents, except during elections.

Medicaid

This section uses a different grant to explore the related question of whether governors can use waivers to influence the amount of formulaically allocated money flowing into a state. Specifically, it focuses on the use of 1915(c) Home and Community Based Services (HCGS) waivers in the states between 1999 and 2005. These waivers were authorized under amendments made to the Social Security Act in 1981 and allow states to deliver both medical and nonmedical long-term care services in non-institutional settings. By waiving certain eligibility and participation requirements, the waivers allow states to target long-term care services at specific populations or regions, reach out to previously un- or under-served populations, and to maintain waiting lists for program participation. By 2008, 283 1915(c) waivers had been granted by DHHS, serving more than 1.2 million Americans in 48 states.[36] On average, over 40% of Medicaid long-term care expenditures are made in programs created under HCBS waivers.[37] These programs, and

Table 3.4   AFDC waivers in the American
states, 1992–1996

Variables	Coefficients
Republican	0.289*
	(0.132)
Election	0.566**
	(0.210)
Republican × election	−0.521*
	(0.259)
Recipients per capita	−5.275**
	(1.800)
Welfare expenditures	401.1
	(278)
Personal income	4.70e-05
	(3.3e-05)
Tax effort	−5.3e-04
	(0.006)
Poverty rate	−.020
	(0.021)
Citizen ideology	0.006
	(0.004)
Governor's power	−0.436**
	(0.146)
Unified government	0.151
	(0.114)
Intercept	0.78
	(0.751)
Year FE significant?	yes
$N =$	245
Pseudo $R^2 =$	0.1
Wald (prob>chi^2) =	106.81 (.0000)

Note: Numbers in parentheses are standard errors.
*p<.05, **p<.01, ***p<.001

the waivers themselves, are supposed to be "cost neutral." Often, however, this requirement can be met via "individual neutrality," meaning that providing home- or community-based care to an *individual* will not cost the Medicaid program more than providing services to that individual in a traditional institutional setting. It does not, therefore, create a strict prohibition against the use of waivers to expand services. There are also no prohibitions against *reducing* costs through the use of 1915(c) waivers.

The core constituents of Republican governors are likely to prefer a reduction or more precise targeting of state health care spending rather than an expansion of Medicaid services, while the co-partisans of a Democratic governor are likely prefer expanded services, all else being equal. This suggests that, if governors are acting strategically, more Republican governors will use waivers to target services to groups they deem more deserving while maintaining or reducing the expenditures. On the other hand, Democrats should use waivers to expand services.[38] If these expectations hold, we should see a positive relationship between waiver participation and federal Medicaid allocations under Democratic governors and a negative or null relationship under Republicans. According to the theory, however, these relationships may weaken or reverse in election years when governors have incentive to use discretion to appeal to a (probably) more moderate median voter.

I test these propositions in an analysis of federal Medicaid allocations to the states between 1999 and 2005. The key independent variable is the number of 1915(c) waiver participants per 1000 population in each state and year. In order to test whether the impact of waivers on Medicaid inflows is different under Republican vs. Democratic governors, the model also contains an indicator of gubernatorial partisanship (1=Republican) and a two-way interaction between that indicator and the measure of participants. In order to estimate the potential moderating effects of elections on the relationship between partisanship, participants, and federal allocations, I also include an indicator of election year and a three-way interaction between that indicator, 1915(c) participants per 1000, and Republican governor. The model also contains the two-way interactions between all constituent terms in order to ensure proper estimation.

In addition to theory-relevant variables and interactions, the model also contains a set of variables that control for alternative explanations for Medicaid allocations to the states. These include measures of state economic conditions, including the unemployment rate and income per capita. It also contains the Federal Medicaid Assistance Percentage, which is heavily based on wealth but provides a more precise measure of the federal match for state Medicaid spending. Next, I include a set of predictors designed to capture the political conditions within a state. Citizen ideology is used to proxy citizen preferences for redistributive programs such as Medicaid, while measures of the governors' formal powers, partisan control of the legislature, and unified vs. divided government pick up the governor's ability to strategically manipulate federal allocations through means other than waivers. Finally, the model contains some potential "supply-side" influences on Medicaid allocations, including indicators of presidential election year and shared partisanship between the White House and the governor's mansion. I also estimate fixed effects for state in order to account for any additional unmeasured influences on Medicaid spending and to ensure that findings reflect relationships *within* rather than across states.

The results from the analysis discussed above are presented in table 3.5. The model is estimated with cross-sectional time series regression with a correction for first order autocorrelation in the dependent variable. The coefficient on the measure of HCBS waiver participants is positive and significant, while the interaction between participants and gubernatorial partisanship is negative and also statistically significant. In general terms, this suggests that having more participants drives up federal Medicaid allocations to the states but that the relationship is negatively moderated when a Republican is governor. The findings also show that the three-way interaction, along with all its constituent terms, fail to reach statistical significance. This suggests that the impact of gubernatorial partisanship on the relationship between waiver participation and Medicaid funding does not change in election years.

Because the three-way interaction is insignificant, we can discuss the interaction between gubernatorial partisanship and waiver participants directly. That interaction suggests that an increase in 1915(c) waiver participants when a Democrat occupies the governor's mansion has a marginal effect of roughly $110 in federal allocations per resident. Alternatively, the coefficient suggests that the same increase under a Republican governor fails to have a statistically significant impact on Medicaid funding inflows. This result is, again, strongly supportive of the assertion that governors use discretion built into the grant-in-aid system to manipulate the amount of formulaic funding flowing into their state in a way that matches the preferences of core constituents. Unlike the model of AFDC, however, the Medicaid result does not suggest that they adapt the use of waivers to appeal to a noncore median voter as elections approach.

Conclusion

This chapter began with an anecdote regarding the refusal of federal monies by U.S. governors and the assertion that this type of behavior was poorly explained by the existing literature on fiscal federalism. It argued that the de-

Table 3.5   Impact of HBCS participation on Medicaid grants to the states, 1999–2005

Variables	Coefficients
Participants	112.7**
	(51.08)
Republican	265.5
	(184.3)
Republican × participants	−78.32*
	(41.58)
Election	236.6
	(237.1)
Election × participants	−23.85
	(57.83)
Republican × election	−180
	(257.2)
Republican × participants × election	23.05
	(57.97)
FMAP	19.79
	(39.42)
Unemployment	36.9
	(37.61)
Personal income	0.0133
	(0.0114)
Presidential election	−0.343
	(42.1)
Same party as president	85.28
	(58.17)
Citizen ideology	12.60**
	(4.985)
Governor's power	69.95
	(217.9)
Unified government	−17.23
	(71.33)
Democratic control of legislature	69.6
	(54.87)
Intercept	−705.2
	(1190.3)
State FE significant?	yes
$N =$	288
$R^2 =$	0.11
$F\,(\text{prob} > F) =$	1.69 (.05)

Note: Numbers in parentheses are standard errors. *$p < .1$, **$p < .05$, ***$p < .01$

cision to accept grants targeted at abstinence education could be explained, however, by the party of the governor and their relative level of electoral security. In other words, it suggested that governors use grants strategically in order to maximize electoral credit by providing goods desired by core constituents and, when necessary, those preferred by noncore median voters.

The analyses presented throughout the remainder of the chapter provide strong evidence for the strategic use of federal grants, with empirical support for the partisan component of the theory being most consistent. States reduced their reliance on Department of Justice grants and increased their participation in Health and Human Services programming in all of the cases where a Democrat replaced a Republican in the 2006 election. In five of the six project grants studied, governors received more funds from programs that match the preferences of their core constituencies. The analyses also confirmed that those relationships hold if we examine applications explicitly, demonstrating that Republican governors not facing an electoral constraint were less likely to apply in both rounds of the Race to the Top competition. Finally, there is evidence that partisan motivations can influence not only the pursuit of project grants but also of discretion to shape the character and scope of much larger formulaically funded programs. Republicans governors not running for reelection were more likely than their Democratic counterparts to receive waivers to impose work requirements and time limits on AFDC recipients. Democrats were more likely to use 1915(c) HCBS waivers to expand Medicaid services, while Republicans were more likely to use waivers to target services more narrowly.

The analyses presented here also provide some evidence, though less consistently, that electoral insecurity can cause governors to pursue grants preferred by voters outside their core constituency. Governors did receive less during election years from grant programs preferred by their core constituencies in three of the six project grants examined, and the impact of elections was in the expected direction in two of the remaining three models. Republican governors running for reelection in 2010 were more likely to apply to both rounds of the RTTT competition when compared to Democrats not facing an electoral constraint. Similarly, Republicans running for reelection were less likely than Democrats who were not running to receive work-requirement and time-limit waivers for their AFDC programs.

Chapter Four

The Strategic Expenditure of Federal Grants

The 2010 Patient Protection and Affordable Care Act (PPACA) mandated that states establish insurance exchanges and provide funding, allocated through the Department of Health and Human Services, to aid in their creation. Nebraska Governor David Heinman quickly became a relatively loud opponent of the new law, declaring that his state would not implement it. Obviously, there were many other, mostly Republican, detractors from the ACA. However, Heinman established himself as somewhat of a standout when he publicly "encouraged" other interests within his state to support a repeal effort with thinly veiled threats of reduced funding for their programs and agencies. Heinman's claims that he had no intention of creating a state-run insurance exchange prompted Nebraska Senator Ben Nelson, who had cast the deciding vote for passage of the Affordable Care Act, to wonder publicly what the governor planned to do with the more than $6 million that DHHS had awarded his state for the planning of an exchange. He went so far as to contact Secretary Sebelius, claiming that the grant was "the taxpayers' money—not the State's—and until there is a plan to put in place an exchange, I don't believe it should be spent."[1]

On the one hand, this was obviously just another volley in the bitter partisan battle that surrounded health care reform. Nonetheless, to the naïve observer it might have given the impression that Nelson believed that grant monies to the states were typically spent solely in the areas targeted by the federal government and that Governor Heinman's actions were therefore some kind of aberration.

The evidence overwhelmingly suggests, however, that this is not the case. In 1996, the General Accounting Office reviewed hundreds of published studies on grants and state expenditures and conducted its own systematic review of over 600 federal grants. In its report to the House Budget Committee, the GAO concluded unequivocally from this review that states were using federal funds for nontargeted functions. More specifically, it reported that the safeguards built into most federal grants are not sufficient "to encourage states to use federal dollars as a supplement rather than a replacement for their own spending on nationally important activities."[2] The agency reached the very same conclusion in a 2004 report on Highway spending. After reviewing the relevant scholarly work and conducting its own sophisticated empirical analysis, it concluded that the "evidence suggests that increased federal highway grants influence states and localities to substitute federal funds for funds they otherwise would have spent on highways."[3] Indeed, the GAO found the same result in a 1996 study of Medicaid, a 1995 investigation of accountability in block grants, and in dozens of other reports made to Congress over the past three decades.

This brief litany, while obviously incomplete, is simply meant to illustrate that scholars and lawmakers alike have long known that state actors sometimes treat federal grants as income—using them to substitute for own-source funds that can then be diverted to provide lower taxes or alternative public goods. Explanations regarding when and why states choose to divert grant funds or to spend them in targeted areas have been consistent over time. These have focused most heavily on the restrictions placed on the expenditure of funds by the federal government, with observers long noting that grants with matching requirements are more likely to induce recipients to supplement rather than supplant own-source funds with grants.[4] As noted above, however, the GAO has suggested that even matching requirements are insufficient to incentivize desired state spending in areas like highway construction and maintenance where states typically spend above the matching limit regardless of federal inflows.[5] Numerous studies, particularly those targeted at policymakers, have also acknowledged the importance of jurisdictional finances in determining grant expenditure, suggesting intuitively that substitution is more likely to occur in times of fiscal hardship.[6] Surprisingly, a relatively limited number of fiscal impact studies examine even the additive effect of jurisdictional political preferences on grant expenditure and an even smaller set have investigated the potential moderating impact of state-level political variables.[7]

As an alternative to the bulk of previous scholarship, I argue that state-level politicians and parties strategically utilize federal grants-in-aid to maximize their chances for reelection or retention of power, within a set of institutional and contextual constraints. More specifically, I argue that, when they are able, members of both parties will use grant monies in order to produce policies that appeal to core constituents and that they may, conditional on electoral security, use grants opportunistically as elections approach in order to increase support among noncore voters.

The previous chapter provided strong evidence that Republicans, in keeping with the preference of core constituents, are more likely to solicit funds that support distributive or developmental, rather than redistributive, policies. It also presented some evidence, albeit weaker, that both parties solicit more grant funding in election relative to nonelection years and that election-year increases in federal grants tend to focus, for Republican governors at least, in areas preferred by noncore voters.

This chapter turns to the question of grant expenditure by state governments. If governors use grants strategically to retain power for themselves and their parties, then we should be able to observe at least some of the following partisan and electoral influences on grant expenditure decisions. If they seek to retain power by using grants to appeal to core constituents, then Republican governors should be more likely to treat grant funding as income that can be diverted to citizens in the form of lower taxes. Under Republicans, grants targeted at redistributive purposes or to enhance regulatory capacity within a jurisdiction should have a lower impact on spending, while those targeted at distributive or developmental purposes should have a higher impact, because of the relative preferences for these types of policies among Republican core voters. If electoral theory is accurate and incumbents act opportunistically as elections approach in an attempt to secure reelection, then incumbents from each party should make grant expenditure decisions that appeal to the median (rather than their core) voter in election years.

Republicans should divert less federal grant funding toward lower taxes and away from redistributive programs, and Democrats should divert less from distributive or development-related spending and more toward lowering the tax burden.

There is another type of expenditure that we might expect to see if governors were using grant funds strategically to increase vote share for themselves or their party. Successfully shepherding a policy agenda through the legislative process is a contributor to executive electoral success, and research suggests that at the national level presidents use federal funding to reward supporters in the legislature. It is reasonable to expect that governors might try to do the same thing. As such, an increased flow of grant aid to legislative districts controlled by the governor's party can provide additional evidence for the partisan hypothesis within the political theory of state-level grant decision making.[8]

The remainder of the chapter is organized around testing these propositions by drawing on multiple datasets, outcome variables, and analytic techniques. The first section examines tax effort in the American states between 1971 and 2005, looking specifically for the degree to which partisan and electoral factors moderate the relationship between changes in grant receipt and changes in tax levels. The second section examines specific grant areas—including Medicaid, Law Enforcement/Corrections, and Highways—to see if federal monies have a larger flypaper effect for relevant state spending in policies preferred by an incumbent's core constituency or when they are facing an election. The chapter then examines governor's State of the State Addresses in order to explore the types of grant expenditure decisions that incumbents claim credit for as well as the timing of credit claiming relative to electoral cycles. As a final test of whether governors spend grant funding strategically in order to produce electoral gain, the chapter examines whether state legislative districts controlled by the governor's party receive a larger share of grant funding flowing into a state.

Grants and Taxes in the American States

Not surprisingly, there has been considerable interest in the correlates of taxation in the U.S. states, and studies have produced relatively consistent results regarding the most important political determinants of state-level tax effort. Recent studies have provided evidence that states headed by Democrats have higher tax effort in both the long and the short run, conditional on levels of institutional control.[9] Other researchers have found that ideological differences also play an important role in the variation in tax effort across the American states, both in terms of the adoption of major taxes and the speed of tax shifts, and that states are significantly less likely to adopt new taxes or raise rates on existing taxes in the year of a gubernatorial election.[10]

Interestingly, however, the literature says very little about the impact of grants-in-aid on state-level taxing decisions. This is surprising because much of the scholarship on grant effectiveness begins with the assumption that there is a relationship between these variables, and most models predict that some portion of grant monies will be returned to jurisdictional citizens in the form of lower taxes.[11] In somewhat of a reversal, this latter body of work has been largely silent about the impact of partisanship and electoral pressures on the relationship between grants and taxes, which, as noted above, has been a central feature of the larger literature on state taxes. Only one study has examined the relationship between federal grants and recipient taxing choices, incorporating some of the political variables suggested in the broader literature on the latter. In previous work, I find that grants exert downward pressure on state taxes but that the relationship is moderated by the level of ideological agreement with the goals of a grant program within a jurisdiction.[12]

This section expands upon and improves my previous model in order to begin testing the general assertion that state-level incumbents spend grant monies strategically in order to achieve electoral goals. Rather than modeling the impact of ideology on expenditure decisions, however, it looks for the influence of gubernatorial party on the relationship between grants and taxes. This is more consistent with the theoretical expectations offered here and also allows for an assessment of the moderating effect of partisanship on *all* grant expenditure choices rather than only on those that are clearly ideological in nature. This model also expands on my previous work by allowing the pressure of an imminent election to interact with other key independent variables. Nicholson-Crotty (2004) includes a measure of gubernatorial election in the model but only as an additive control. In contrast, the expectations offered above require that elections be allowed to moderate the relationship between grants and taxes as well as the relationship between party, grants, and taxes via a three-way interaction. Finally, the model of taxes presented here offers an advantage over previous studies because it extends the period under study to 2005. Previous work analyzed data only from 1971 to 1996, effectively missing the so-called Republican Revolution of the mid-1990s when that party took control of a majority of governor's mansions for the first time since 1972.

Variables

The key dependent variable in this section is tax effort. Scholars suggest that when studying taxing choices, a general measure of the amount of state wealth that government is willing to claim as revenue is superior to an examination of increases or decreases in any individual tax category.[13] In other words, they suggest that overall tax effort or burden should be conceptualized as the amount the state collects relative to the total amount it *could* collect. There are two primary approaches to calculating a state's fiscal capacity. The most widely used of these is the RTS, or representative tax system, which measures capacity as the amount of revenue that a state would collect if it taxed at a standard or "representative" rate across 21 different types of taxes and abolished all breaks, exemptions, and loopholes.[14] Though the RTS approach has been widely adopted, there have been a number of criticisms.[15]

In response to these and other criticisms, scholars have offered alternative means of determining tax capacity and effort. Most notable among these is the Total Taxable Resources (TTR) approach developed by the U.S. Treasury Department, which basically calculates state tax capacity as Gross State Product minus those components of GSP that are not taxable (e.g., social insurance contributions) but plus income flows not recorded in GSP (e.g., earnings of out-of-state residents).[16] In the TTR approach, tax effort is the proportion of total *available* resources claimed by the government through taxes.

The biggest problem with both measures, from the perspective of this project, is the limited time frames for which they have been calculated for all 50 states. Through a somewhat torturous path, the RTS measure is available from 1971 to 1996.[17] Using data obtained from the Treasury Department, John Mikesell has constructed the longest TTR series available for all 50 states. Unfortunately, his measure is only available from 1981 to 2003.

Because the Advisory Council for Intergovernmental Relations (ACIR) and the Mikesell measures are constructed in fundamentally different ways, and because they do not correlate highly in the period of overlap (Pearsons R = .47), they cannot be combined into a single series. It is important to analyze the relationship between grants and tax effort over as long a period as possible, however, in order to avoid bias arising from a failure to observe key changes in the position and functioning of state governments over the past four decades. In order to reconcile these two realities, I offer two analyses of tax effort here. The first models the RTS-based measure available between 1971 and 1996, and the second estimates the determinants of the TTR-based series from 1981 to 2003. Diagnostics indicate that both tax series are non-stationary, so the variables are differenced prior to analysis. Because there is not a theoretical reason to believe that the level of federal grants would influence the year-to-year change in taxation, I also difference all continuous variables on the right-hand side of the equations.[18] Both models also include state-level fixed effects in order to ensure that all comparisons are between governors of different parties within the same state, rather than across states.[19]

The measures of tax effort that I model in this analysis are superior to older measures of taxes used in this literature.[20] However, in order to confirm that results are not a function of this operational choice, table 4.1 also contains a model of taxes per capita, which more closely approximates measures used in prominent studies of tax effort.[21]

The key independent variables capture grants, party, elections, and the interaction of these variables. The measure of grants includes only funds categorized as grants-in-aid by the Catalogue of Federal Domestic Assistance, including all project, cooperative agreement, formulaic, and block grants received by each state in each year. The measure excludes all other forms of federal transfer, including insurance, direct payments to individuals, procurement contracts, loans. The measure is normalized by population (i.e., per capitized). It is differenced in the first two models, while the level value of the dependent variable is used in the third model. Gubernatorial party is captured with a dichotomous indicator coded 1 for Republicans and 0 otherwise, while elections are coded 1 if a governor is running for reelection and 0 otherwise. For purposes of hypothesis testing, the models also include a two-way interaction between gubernatorial party and differenced grants as well as a three-way interaction between gubernatorial party, change in grant funding, and election year. Because estimating three-way interactions properly requires the inclusion of all three pairs of two-way interactions, the models also include the interactions between election and grants, and between election and gubernatorial party.

In addition to these independent variables, the models discussed in this section also include control variables suggested by the theoretical story offered here and in previous research on state tax effort. I have suggested that a governor's power to convert grants into political resources such as lower taxes is conditional on several institutional features of the state. In order to capture these, the models discussed below include an indicator of Democratic control of both houses of the legislature as well as an indicator of unified control by one party of both the legislature and the statehouse. They also include the measure of formal gubernatorial powers developed by Thad Beyle.

In order to control for alternative explanations for state taxing decisions, the models include a measure of the percentage of a state's population living in urban areas, which should correlate positively with tax effort.[22] They also include an indicator of whether a state has taxing and spending limits, passed via statute or initiative. Some evidence suggests that these restrictions on state government may decrease taxation, and the measure should therefore be negatively correlated with the dependent variables. The models also control for the wealth within a state based on previous research which suggests that taxation, and presumably an increase in the share of state resources claimed for government revenue, becomes more attractive to lawmakers as available wealth increases.[23] Because I need a measure of wealth not included in the calculation of tax capacity used in either measure of tax effort, the models include income per capita. I also include the percentage of total general revenue originating from local sources on the right-hand side because some states make significantly greater demands on local government for the provision of services than do others, which has been shown to influence the effort that the state expends in collecting revenue.[24] Finally, I include an indicator of the annual unemployment rate based on the assumption that lawmakers will be less likely to raise taxes when more citizens are out of work. For those models with differenced dependent variables (1 and 2), continuous controls are differenced, while the level of each control is used in the third model.

The findings from analyses of state tax effort are presented in table 4.1. The model of the RTS-based measure (1971–1996) is in column 1, while the second column contains the model of the TTR effort variable (1981–2003). Results of the mode of taxes per capita are presented in column 3. As noted above, the first two analyses first difference models with state-level fixed effects, and both correct for first-order autocorrelation that remains in the differenced dependent variables.

Table 4.1   Grants, gubernatorial party, and tax effort in the American states

Variables	RTS	TTR	TaxPC
Grants	0.001	1.79e-06**	78.612**
	(.002)	(7.93e-07)	(26.53)
Republican governor	−0.687*	3.92e-04	165.706*
	(.388)	(.4.53e-04)	(92.84)
Election	0.485	−6.37e-05	155.132
	(.486)	(6.6e-05)	(106.617)
Republican governor × grants	−0.007**	−5.11e-06*	−27.273*
	(.004)	(3.01e-06)	(33.00)
Republican governor × election	0.078	−0.001	−252.984*
	(.766)	(.000)	(138.167)
Election × grants	−0.007	−1.06e-5*	−23.954
	(.006)	(6.09e-06)	(16.15)
Republican governor × election × grants	0.012	2.05e-5**	38.943*
	(.010)	(1.03e-05)	(20.88)
Tax/expenditure limits	0.202	−1.53e-05	15.727
	(.461)	(5.63e-04)	(16.01)
Personal income (per 1,000)	0.001	1.18e-04	0.005***
	(.001)	(8.37e-05)	(.002)
Unemployment	−0.109	−6.27e-05	−10.892***
	(.098)	(1.54e-04)	(3.54)
Democratic control of legislature	5.40e-06	1.2e-09	−.262
	(.599)	(2.5e-08)	(8.39)
Unified government	−0.383	4.2e-05	7.978
	(.453)	(2.9e-06)	(6.36)
Government power	.023	−.0001	−23.803
	(.024)	(.0001)	(23.65)
Term limits	−0.789	−0.001**	3.382
	(.545)	(5.54e-04)	(7.21)
Intercept	0.241	−7.73e-05	3927.53***
	(.353)	(3.18e-04)	(29.32)
$N =$	1191	1050	1029
$R^2 =$	0.02	0.02	.41
$F =$	1.41	1.72	15.58

Note: Models include state fixed effects. Numbers in parentheses are standard errors. *p<.1, **p<.05, ***p<.01

Turning to the first model, it is important to note that the three-way inter-action between Governor's party, Grants, and Election year is not statistically significant, suggesting that governors do not change the amount of federal money diverted into private benefits in election years. Because of the interactive nature of the model, this bears directly on the interpretation of remaining effects. As expected, having a Republican governor is negatively associated with changes in tax effort.[25] The main effect for grants is not statistically significant, suggesting that a change in federal monies is not associated with a change in tax effort under Democratic governors.[26] However, the interaction term for grants and gubernatorial party is both negative and significant, suggesting that federal grants do exert downward pressure on state tax effort in states headed by a Republican. Substantively, the result suggests that a 1-standard deviation increase in federal grants decreases the change in tax effort in a state by .2-standard deviation under a Republican governor. The RTS measure of tax effort or changes in it do not have a great deal of substantive meaning, but we can note that a 1-standard deviation change in grants under a Republican governor exerts more downward pressure on tax effort than does switching from a Democratic to a Republican governor!

The model of the Total Taxable Resources (TTR) measure of tax effort in the American states between 1980 and 2003 is presented in column 2. We can note initially that many right-hand side variables perform differently in this model—speaking to the substantive differences between the RTS and TTR methods for calculating tax effort and the different time frame. Most interesting, however, is the fact that both the two-way and the three-way interactions are significant in this model. The coefficient for grants, which here represents grants awarded to states headed by Democrats in nonelection years, is positive and significant. Though the substantive impact is very small, this suggests that an increase in grants is associated with an increase in tax effort under these conditions. The interaction between gubernatorial party and grants is negative, indicating that grants awarded to Republican governors in nonelection years exert downward pressure on taxes relative to grants received by Democrats in the same state in nonelection years. Finally, the three-way interaction term is positive and significant, which suggests that governors within a state change the amount of federal money they divert into lower taxes in election years.

The substantive impact of the three-way interaction is easier to interpret graphically, and is, in this case, the most intuitive way to plot expected values. I have also attempted to increase the clarity of presentation by separating the plots by party. Figure 4.1 presents the expected value of the change in tax effort at different values of change in grants for Republicans in both election and nonelection years. The results suggest that in nonelection years an increase in grants is significantly associated with a reduction in tax ef-

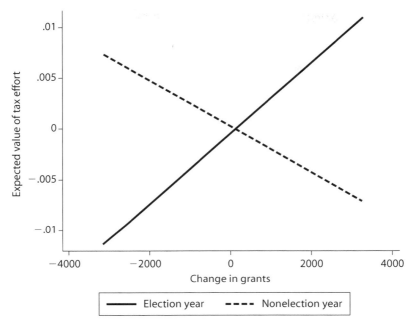

Figure 4.1 Tax effort (TTR) and the interaction of grants, elections, and Republican governor

fort at all values of the independent variable. Alternatively, the figure suggests that grants do not have a significant impact on tax effort in years when a Republican is running for reelection. Not surprisingly, for Democrats the pattern is reversed. The expected changes in tax effort, given annual changes in grant revenue under Democratic governors, are plotted in figure 4.2. The figure suggests that an increase in grant revenue is associated with a negative change in tax effort in election years and that grants are positively associated with tax effort in nonelection years.

The final model of tax effort, measured with taxes per capita, is presented in the third column of table 4.1. First, it is interesting to note that this model has a much higher R^2 (.40) than the previous two, likely because the dependent variable is not differenced. The control variables perform largely as the literature suggests they should. State wealth is positively associated with tax effort, while unemployment rates and total population are negatively correlated with the dependent variable. The results from this model are supportive of both the partisan and electoral hypotheses. Specifically, they suggest that

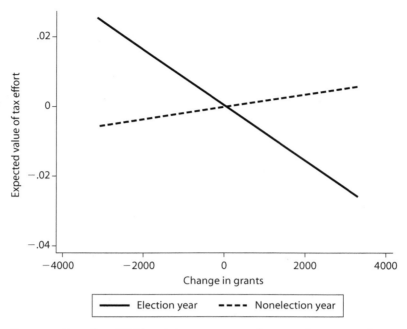

Figure 4.2 Tax effort (TTR) and the interaction of grants, elections, and Democratic governor

grants have a larger positive impact on tax effort under Democrats than on Republicans in nonelection years. In election years, however, the difference between governors from the two parties disappears.

These analyses of three very distinct measures of state tax effort (RTS v. TTR v. Taxes per capita) provide consistent support for the assertion that governors use grants-in-aid to provide economic policies and outcomes that appeal to core voters and some support for the expectation that they will act opportunistically as elections approach to appeal to noncore voters. In all three models, Republicans, whose constituents expect and reward smaller government and lower taxes, were more likely to divert federal funds into private goods. The RTS model suggests that Republicans use grants to lower taxes regardless of whether it is an election year. It suggests that there is not a significant relationship between grants and taxes under Democratic governors. The TTR and Total Taxes per capita models also suggest that Republicans divert grants into lower taxes but indicate that they are only willing to do so in nonelection years. The expected values generated by the TTR model also indicate that tax effort correlates positively with grants under Democratic governors when they are not running for reelection but that the relationship turns negative in election years.

Grants and Spending on Specific Policies in the American States

All this discussion of the diversion of grant funds to private goods, while informative, belies the fact that jurisdictions also use federal funds to reduce the price of public goods, allowing them to purchase more than they would have been able to in the absence of the grant. Indeed, the modal study suggests that the *majority* of federal dollars produce this effect. There is more to know, however, about why recipients sometimes choose to avail themselves of the price effect of grants and at other times choose to treat them as income. This is the just the logical inverse of the question posed at the outset of the previous section on tax effort, but asking it in this way allows us to go further into the motivations of state-level actors. More specifically, it pushes us to ask not only why jurisdictions spend grants the way they do but also why they spend some types of grants differently than others.

The dominant explanations for these decisions in the literature have already been reviewed in depth elsewhere in this and previous chapters. These focus heavily on grant conditions, the degree to which the federal government monitors a particular stream of funding, and the discretion that these factors afford recipients when making spending decisions. Only one study has explicitly examined the ways the political preferences of state-level actors influence their grant expenditure choices. I have argued elsewhere that the agreement with the goals of targeted programs helps to determine state spending and demonstrates that Medicaid funds have a larger impact on state health spending in liberal states, while the Byrne Anti-Narcotics grant stimulates more jurisdictional spending in conservative states.[27]

The data here expands on and improves my earlier analysis in order to test the theoretical proposition that governors use grants strategically to maximize partisan and, ultimately, electoral benefits. The primary way that it does so is by allowing an approaching election, and thus electoral security, to moderate the impact of partisan preferences on the grant–spending relationship. It also examines jurisdictional spending decisions in a broader array of grant areas, including Medicaid, highways, and law enforcement and corrections.

Finally, it investigates spending over a longer time period, extending it to 2005, thus allowing it to include the period during and after Republicans gained a majority of governor's mansions around the country, which was excluded from previous work.

This section is organized by grant type, with each subsection providing a brief description of the program in question, specifying the appropriate model, and then briefly discussing the results from an analysis of the grant's impact on the relevant category of state spending. A more in-depth discussion of the results follows these subsections.

Medicaid

Medicaid is the nation's largest public health insurance program, providing health and long-term care coverage to 52 million low-income people in 2004. It is also one of the largest domestic federal grant programs, with expenditures totaling more than $205 billion in 2007. In the average state, the portion of Medicaid funded by the state from own-source revenue comprises 16% of total outlays, making it the second-largest expenditure category.[28] Medicaid is a jointly funded program whereby states match federal contributions. The matching rate, or Federal Medical Assistance Percentage (FMAP), ranges between 50% and 77%, depending on the state. As noted above, that match is intended to ensure that Medicaid funds supplement rather than supplant state-level spending on health, but there is considerable evidence that significant diversions continue.

Medicaid is a classic example of redistributive policy, providing benefits to persons at or near the poverty line paid for via taxation of wealthier citizens. Republican voters, and the politicians they elect to serve in government, have a well-documented distaste for these types of policies. As a result, the theoretical model laid out in this book suggests that Republican gubernatorial incumbents will spend less federal Medicaid money on targeted expenditures than do their Democratic counterparts. It also suggests, however, that the desire to retain power may lead Republicans to increase the amount spent on the provision of health care to the poor as elections approach in an attempt to appeal to noncore voters.

The model discussed here tests for the impact of gubernatorial partisanship and elections on the stimulative effect of Medicaid grants on state health care spending. The party and elections variables are coded in the same manner as in previous analyses. The primary independent variable is inflation adjusted per capitized Medicaid funds awarded to each state in each year. The variable is non-stationary. As a result it is differenced, and the model is estimated as a fixed-effects, first-differences model identical to the one employed in the previous section. For the purposes of hypothesis testing, it includes the two-way interaction between Medicaid grants and gubernatorial party and a three-way interaction between grants, party, and an indicator of the governor seeking reelection as well as the remaining two constituent interaction terms. Control variables are similar to those in the tax effort models and include an indicator of partisan control of both chambers in the legislature, an indicator of unified government, measures of executive fragmentation and formal power, income per capita, the unemployment rate, and percentage urban. In addition, the model controls for the Federal Medicaid Assistance Percentage, or the match rate that the federal government provides for state spending. The FMAP is heavily dependent on personal income within a state, but it provides a more precise control for the amount spending should increase if states are using Medicaid grants exclusively for the price effect and not treating them as income.

The results from the analysis are presented in the first column of table 4.2. The two-way interaction between gubernatorial party and Medicaid grants is jointly significant. Despite the multiple interactions, the substantive findings from this model are easier to interpret because the independent and dependent variables are measured on the same metric. Those findings suggest that, after controlling for other factors, a $1 increase in Medicaid produces a 60-cent increase in state health spending under Democratic governors in nonelection years. Alternatively, a $1 increase received by a Republican governor not running for reelection results in only 49 cents in own-source spending. To put this in perspective, even after removing California and New York as outliers, the average state received more than a $700 million increase in federal Medicaid funding between 2009 and 2010. If that "average" state were headed by a Democrat not running for reelection, that federal money would buy a $420 million increase in own-source expenditures. Alternatively, if it were headed by a Republican also not facing an electoral constraint, that same increase would only produce $343 million more in state spending. That is a difference of more than $77 million, and it is important to remember that it arises from a prediction that includes state fixed effects and explicitly controls for FMAP and other influences on state expenditures.

The three-way interaction between party, grants, and running for reelec-

Table 4.2   Grants, gubernatorial party, and grant expenditure in the American states

Variables	Medicaid	Highways	Corrections
Δ Grants	0.598***	0.612***	−0.007
	(.048)	(.079)	(.354)
Republican governor	28.784	−4.833	−0.003
	(19.958)	(3.186)	(.038)
Election	44.158*	−7.847	−0.035
	(.25.587)	(6.323)	(.065)
Republican governor × Δ grants	−.108*	.232**	0.354***
	(.061)	(.101)	(.042)
Republican governor × election	2.648	−.271	0.055
	(38.209)	(7.446)	(.095)
Election × Δ grants	−.307**	.054	0.096
	(.159)	(.054)	(.096)
Republican governor × election × Δ grants	−.262*	0.264	−0.401**
	(.149)	(.298)	(.185)
Urbanization	2.435	0.124	−2.08e-04
	(1.245)	(.166)	(.002)
Δ Personal income	0.001	0.002*	3.65e-06
	(.004)	(.001)	(1.11e-05)
Δ unemployment	−2.412	−0.225	−0.007
	(5.861)	(1.145)	(.014)
Democratic control of legislature	5.789	2.109	−.033*
	(10.636)	(1.683)	(.018)
Unified government	5.009	−4.959*	0.026
	(18.265)	(3.024)	(.037)
Government power	41.203	−0.059	−0.034
	(30.447)	(4.230)	(.051)
Term limits	32.022	−8.616	0.016
	(29.053)	(6.031)	(.076)
Δ FMAP	−11.602**		
	(5.858)		
Δ VMT		−0.007	
		(.007)	
Intercept	−454.607	1.79	0.344
	(96.321)	(19.107)	(.239)
$N =$	1614	1614	1614
$R^2 =$	0.24	0.16	0.12
$F =$	29.87	18.58	17.78

Note: Models include state fixed effects. Numbers in parentheses are standard errors. *$p<.1$, **$p<.05$, ***$p<.01$

tion independently reaches the threshold for significance. Contrary to expectations, however, the results suggest that the flypaper effect of Medicaid grants actually drops as elections approach for governors from *both* parties.

Highways

The second column in table 4.2 focuses on Highway Planning and Construction grants. Each year states are "authorized" to obligate funds under the auspices of this multi-year federal authorization. The national government helps to produce a wide variety of transportation projects via Federal Highway Administration (FHWA) funds, including those under the Interstate Maintenance Program, the National Highway System Program, the Surface Transportation Program, the Highway Bridge Replacement and Rehabilitation Program, the Congestion Mitigation and Air Quality Control Program, and numerous others.[29] Federal aid for these individual programs is apportioned by formula, using factors relevant to the particular program. After those computations are made, additional funds are distributed so that each state receives an amount that ensures some degree of return on its contributions to the Highway Account of the Highway Trust Fund. The guaranteed rate of return has varied over time. States are also increasingly augmenting their funds via innovative financing programs such as State Infrastructure Banks, Credit Leveraging, and others. Highway funds typically have a matching requirement, but that condition is less consequential than in other programs because the states typically spend a good deal more in own-source funds than the matching percentage.

Unlike Medicaid, which has a clear redistributive focus, FHWA spending is a classic distributive policy. Revenues are collected from a wide tax base, both within and outside a specific state, and then distributed in a way that benefits a large number of citizens. Research suggests that these are the policies that Republicans and their constituents are likely to give high priority.[30]

The dependent variable in this model is the annual change in per capitized, inflation-adjusted, own-source highway spending, which includes disbursements from current revenues or loans for construction, maintenance, interest and principal payments on highway bonds, transfers to local units, transactions by state toll authorities, and miscellaneous expenditures.[31] As in previous models, the independent variables capture gubernatorial party, election year, and the annual change in the grant—in this case, Highway Planning and Construction. The model includes a set of controls similar to those discussed above as well as a measure of total Vehicle Miles Traveled (VMT) within each state and year, which is the best generalized proxy of the need for state highway spending.

In the analysis of state highway expenditures presented in table 4.2, the three-way interaction is not significant, which suggests that incumbents from different parties do not make different grant-expenditure decisions in election years. The two-way interaction between gubernatorial party and grants is significant, however, indicating that governors from different parties spend grants differently. Substantively, the results suggest that a $1 increase in Highway Planning and Construction funds received by Democratic incumbents results in a 61-cent increase in state spending. When received by a Republican governor from the same state, that dollar produces an 84-cent increase in targeted own-source expenditures. The average state received an increase of $73 million in highway funding between 2008 and 2009, meaning that, all else being equal, awarding money to a Republican rather than a Democrat paid an average dividend of $27 million to the federal government in terms of state-level investment in roadways.

Law Enforcement and Corrections

The stimulative effect of justice-related grants on state-level law enforcement and corrections spending is shown in the third column of table 4.2. The "grant" in this case is actually an aggregation of all justice-related grants awarded in each state and year. The largest of these programs include the Byrne Anti-Narcotics initiative, the Violent Offender Incarceration and Truth in Sentencing program, a broad category of Criminal Justice Discretionary Grants, and Community Policing, but there have been an average of almost 30 justice-related grants each year in the time period under study. Even combined, however, these grants total less than one-fifth of federal highway awards and less than one-tenth of federal Medicaid funding in the average state and year. Thus, in order to reliably examine the impact of grants on state spending in this partisan and electorally charged issue area, it is necessary to combine them.

This is not ideal, of course, because we might imagine members of different parties having different incentives to spend, depending on the specific character of the justice-related grant. This is less worrisome in Department of Justice grants than it might be in other areas because of the relatively ideologically consistent nature of the programs funded by the agency.[32] However, to the degree to which such divergence does occur, it should simply introduce additional noise in the model, making it more difficult to find significant results. Another factor complicating the aggregation of justice-related grants is the fact that some have matching formulas, while others do not.[33] This means that it is impossible to predict what the stimulative effect of $1 in aggregate money *should* be. Nonetheless, if expenditure decisions are influenced by partisan and electoral concerns, then we should still be able to observe a difference in the flypaper effect between parties and in election versus nonelection years.

The dependent variable in this model is the annual change in state-level law enforcement and corrections spending, adjusted for inflation and normalized by population. The independent variables are the same as in previous models, with the obvious caveat that all relevant interactions now include federal justice grants. The control variables are also identical, except that this model does not include the FMAP included in the model of Medicaid or the measure of VMT from the highways model because these are likely irrelevant to state spending decisions in this area.

In the results from the analysis of state corrections spending presented in the third column of table 4.2, the two-way interaction between gubernatorial party and the annual change in justice grants is positive and significant, as is the three-way interaction between grants, party, and elections. As such, the coefficient on the main effect for grants, which is not significant (and substantively quite small), suggests than a $1 increase in justice-related grants has no stimulative effect on state-level corrections spending when received by a Democratic incumbent in a nonelection year. This is a little surprising, given that roughly half of the largest programs included in the aggregate grant measure have a matching requirement, and may suggest that Democrats are supplanting own-source with federal funds. The positive and significant interaction between the party of the governor and the change in grants suggests that the same $1 of federal money has a very different impact when received by a Republican governor in the same state who is also not facing reelection. There the results indicate that an increase in justice-related grants is used to leverage about 35 cents in additional state spending on corrections and law enforcement. Interestingly, however, the significant three-way interaction suggests that the differential impact of these grants across gubernatorial party reverses itself during election years. The coefficient suggests that $1 of federal corrections and law enforcement spending actually results in a reduction of own-source spending by Republicans facing an election. This, again, suggests that federal funds are likely being substituted for state spending. The most interesting thing about the result is that the election-year substitution is taking place despite the likely agreement between the governor and the goals of the program to be funded by the grant.

Summary of Grant Expenditure Findings

The models discussed above provide consistent support for a partisan theory of grant expenditure which suggests that governors will spend grants in order to deliver benefits to core constituents. In all three cases, the flypaper effect was larger for grants targeting policy areas preferred by the core constituency of the governor. Medicaid funds had a larger stimulative effect on own-source spending when received by Democrats, while Highway and Justice grants were associated with more state-level expenditures in those policy areas under Republican governors.

The results also provide some, though significantly weaker, evidence for the electoral theory of grant expenditure, the idea that governors spend grants opportunistically to attract noncore voters as elections approach. The model of state law enforcement / corrections spending suggests that federal grants had stimulative effect when received by Republican governors who were not running for reelection but that the flypaper effect dissipated completely in election years. By contrast, the analysis of state health care spending suggests that Democrats spent less federal Medicaid money in the targeted area in election versus nonelection years, but the stimulative effect on state health care spending also decreased under Republican governors in election years. This last result is obviously counter to the expectations produced by electoral theory.

Gubernatorial Credit Claiming for Grant Expenditure

This chapter has examined taxing and spending in order to understand strategic choices regarding grant expenditure. We now focus on what governors *say* about those choices. More specifically, we examine instances of credit claiming regarding the expenditure of federal monies. Obviously, this approach is limited to investigating cases when governors are taking advantage of the price effect of grants, because they will probably not publicly admit diverting federal dollars from targeted public goods. Nonetheless, it also offers advantages over an examination of the relationship between grant receipt and spending. Those advantages arise from the more direct linkage between credit claiming and perceived political advantage. Politicians advertise behavior or accomplishments to constituents when they believe that doing so will help them to achieve political goals.[34] Governors claim credit for receiving and spending federal grant money in a particular area because they believe that it will help them or their party win or retain voters. As such, if we observe governors claiming credit for expenditures in a way that is consistent with the assertions outlined at the beginning of this chapter, we can have greater faith that those decisions are designed to produce electoral advantage.

Obviously, there are a variety of places to examine credit-claiming behavior by governors, including press accounts, campaign activities, and speeches. This section focuses on State of the State Addresses between 2000 and 2008 because governors' addresses to the legislatures in their states have a number of advantages over other potential sources of credit-claiming data. They are available for all 50 states in every year or every other year, depending on the state. Thus, they occur in both election and nonelection years, unlike most campaign activities. The format and length of the speeches are roughly comparable across states and years. As such, the space available for credit claiming regarding federal spending is more comparable than in other public addresses, which vary dramatically in frequency and length. Finally, State of the State Addresses are a valuable source of data on the motivations underlying grant expenditure credit claiming because they have been validated in previous work as "an excellent direct measure of governors' preferences, values, and ideology."[35]

There are two types of information on grant expenditure that can be culled from governors' annual addresses. The first of these is quantitative and reveals if there is a *pattern* of credit-claiming behavior that matches the partisan and electoral hypotheses offered earlier in the chapter. The second, and perhaps more interesting, is qualitative and offers insight into the ways that *individual* governors from different parties talk about grant decisions and the expenditure choices they highlight in election versus nonelection years.

For the quantitative analysis, I code the number of times a governor claims credit for spending grant funds in policy areas that are classically associated with either the Democratic or the Republican parties. The former includes expanding health care coverage, increasing educational access or quality for low-income children, and increasing environmental regulation. The measure ranges between 0 and 2, and in most years governors do not claim credit for spending grants in any of these areas. "Republican" spending areas include reducing welfare rolls, increasing highway expenditure, increasing veterans benefits, more spending on law enforcement, and economic development activities. Again, the measure takes on a value of 0 in most years, but ranges from 0 to 2. Issues such as higher education spending, improving efficiency in health care delivery, disaster relief, and programs to expand home ownership were not coded as either Democrat or Republican because they may be attractive to the constituents of either or both parties.

The degree of precision possible in quantitative analyses of these data is relatively limited. It is imprudent to estimate state fixed effects because the maximum number of observations per unit is eight. Additionally, these are panel data, but the use of traditional cross-sectional time series methods is complicated by the fact that some states only have an address every other year, creating unbalanced panels. The fact that some governors do not speak every year creates a potential selection effect because they cannot be consistently observed in the sample. This is particularly problematic in states such as Arkansas that do not have State of the State addresses in gubernatorial election years. Dealing with all of these issues with this sample size and the distribution of these dependent variables is difficult or impossible. In order to avoid bias and a sense of false precision, therefore, I offer the simplest analysis of the data—a comparison of proportions. Readers should treat these analyses with caution and view them as suggestive only.

The findings from simple comparisons of the relative frequency with which governors claim credit for different types of spending accord fairly well with the expectations outlined at the outset of this chapter. Democrats not running for reelection claimed credit for spending grants on "liberal" purposes in 8.2% of their speeches. Alternatively, Republicans talked about grant expenditure in those areas only 6% of the time.[36] In election years, the pattern of credit claiming on redistributive grant expenditure is reversed. In those years, Democratic governors talk about spending federal money for liberal policies 4% of the time, while Republicans facing reelection do so in 11% of their speeches. Republicans not facing reelection were more likely to claim credit for grant expenditures (15%) on distributive and developmental policies than were Democrats (12.5%).[37] As expected, Democrats significantly increased the percentage of speeches in which they claimed credit for this type of spending (17%) during election years. However, the results suggest that Republicans *also* drew more attention to grant expenditure on distributive policies when facing reelection, which was counter to expectations.

So the quantitative results suggest consistent evidence for a partisan theory of grant expenditure and mixed support for the assertion that incumbents will opportunistically claim credit for different types of federal expenditure as elections approach. We can gain another perspective by looking at some specific examples of how credit claiming changed when a governor from a different party took over, or when incumbents entered an election year. For example, Tony Knowles, the two-term Democratic governor of Alaska from 1994 to 2002 used his State of the State address to highlight the expenditure of federal grants twice, and both instances were for programs typically preferred by Democratic constituents. In 1999, he discussed use of federal money to expand Alaska's children's health insurance program. In 2001, he focused part of his address on the plight of portions of the state's indigenous population but reminded constituents that "thanks to $523 million in state and federal funds, nearly 70 percent now have clean water and sewage disposal."[38]

Republican Frank Murkowski won the race for Governor of Alaska in 2002, campaigning primarily on his very conservative congressional voting record. His State of the State speeches seemed tailored to the same constituency that elected him. He claimed credit for using federal monies only once, and did so to highlight *less* expenditure on traditional liberal programs. Specifically, he pointed out to constituents that "in the last year alone, we've reduced our welfare rolls by 9 percent" and that "Alaska was the recipient of a 3.2-million-dollar federal bonus for its welfare-to-work success." The end of Murkowski's term was riddled with scandal, and he lost the 2006 election to the mayor of a little-known (at the time) town called Wasilla. Sarah Palin was also a Republican, of course; and she claimed credit for grant expenditures two times in 2007 and 2008, continuing to emphasize spending choices that appealed to the core constituents of her party. She claimed credit for economic development activities, reminding voters that her administration "had redirected $50 million in federal funds obtained by Senator Stevens and our Delegation to revitalize the [salmon] industry." She also celebrated additional federal funds that she had secured for highways in the state. "All combined," she claimed, "our FY07 transportation budget is $1.3 billion, of which $873 million is federal funds—for those who are adding it up."

Alaska is not the only state where there is clear evidence of a change in grant expenditure credit claiming after a partisan shift in the governor's mansion. Republican Bob Taft was elected governor of Ohio in 1998 and again in 2002. Economic development, particularly in the area of biomedical research, was a key component of both terms, and he used the majority of his grant expenditure credit claiming to highlight accomplishments related to that goal.[39] In 2003, he reminded constituents, "We've awarded $45 million through the Technology Action and Biomedical Research funds, generating millions more in federal and private funds." Two years later, the governor made the similar claim that "we've helped attract federal funds for Cleveland's Center for Stem Cell and Regenerative Medicine, the Fuel Cell Prototyping Center in Canton, and a center for alternative energy in Toledo." Finally, in 2006, he told the citizens of Ohio: "We're attracting more federal research dollars than ever before, leading to more good jobs for our college graduates."

In 2006, Taft was term-limited out of office and Democrat Ted Strickland took over. Though Strickland received the endorsement of numerous law enforcement organizations and some support from Republicans during his campaign, his core constituency was the state's registered Democrats.[40] Not surprisingly, he catered consistently to that constituency throughout his tenure, increasing health care coverage for pregnant women, capping insurance costs on pre-existing conditions, defunding school voucher programs, and making one of the largest investments in "green" school construction in the nation.[41] The references to federal grants in Strickland's State of the State speeches also provide insight into the group of voters he was targeting. In 2007 he highlighted the federal government's Work Force Investment Act, which provides job training primarily to low-skilled workers, and bemoaned the fact that Ohio was "51st in making use of those funds." In 2009, along with highlighting the importance of the Stimulus Bill to Ohio residents, Strickland noted that his administration had secured federal approval and funds "to offer coverage to Ohio children from families with incomes up to 300 percent of the poverty line." He went on to point out that "with funding provided in this budget, we will soon be able to say that health care coverage is available to every child in Ohio."

Along with these examples of credit claiming targeted at core constituents, there is also evidence that governors sometimes change the types of grants they claim credit for as elections approach. For one example of such behavior, we can return to Ohio. As noted above, Governor Taft consistently claimed credit for seeking, receiving, and spending federal grants for stimulating growth in high-technology industries, often located in the state's suburbs and benefiting primarily the college-educated and higher-skilled workforce. When running for reelection in 2002, he continued to focus on economic development, but for a very different constituency. "Last year," Taft told voters, "we doubled funding for economic development in Appalachia, and we'll keep that commitment again this year. We'll work to attract even more federal funds to distressed counties."

Comparable examples of election-year changes in credit claiming can be found in other states. Bill Owens served as Colorado's governor from 1999 to 2007, making traditional Republican issues of tax cuts and infrastructure the centerpieces of his administrations.[42] During his second term, discussions of grant expenditure in his State of the State Addresses seemed targeted at that constituency. He promised to do "a better job of drawing down on all available federal grants and matching funds" for criminal justice and education spending, and he reminded voters that his administration had "directed $4.2 million in federal funds to establish a statewide information-security initiative." When running for his second term, however, Owens's reminder to voters that "Colorado received $142 million from the federal government last spring in unemployment insurance funding" was likely focused at a different constituency.

Grants and the Legislature

This chapter has provided considerable evidence that governors spend, and claim credit for spending, grants on public and private benefits in a way that seems designed to increase electoral security. Governors might also use this resource to help members of their own party in the legislature as another mechanism for improving the electoral fortunes of themselves and their party. This supposition is consistent with Morehouse, who argue convincingly that incumbents must work to maintain and grow their party coalition, through the distribution of "rewards and punishments" available to them, in order to ensure the success of their legislative agenda. In keeping with Morehouse's previous work, they find that governors are more successful in securing the votes of their own party members and building coalitions across party lines when they have greater inducements at their disposal.[43]

Existing work at the state level has not directly investigated the ways governors use the distribution of federal grants-in-aid to help them build these coalitions and garner legislative success.[44] However, there is work on distributive politics at the national level that can guide expectations regarding the behavior of governors. Presidents are expected to have the power to influence the distribution of grants because they make the initial budget proposal.[45] Furthermore, they are assumed to have the incentive to do so because they want to (1) reward members of Congress for legislative support, (2) ensure the electoral success of members of their party (and by extension themselves), and (3) strengthen the party as a whole.[46] Most importantly, scholars have found considerable support for the assertion that presidents do, in fact, use federal spending to improve the fortunes of individuals from their party.[47]

Given the partisan and electoral incentives that scholars assume underlie these activities, there is absolutely no reason to believe that governors would not also use grants to improve their position with legislators. There is also ample reason to believe that they should be *at least* as able to make use of federal funds as their national counterpart. Governors may have an even greater "proposer" power because they face less-active legislatures that often have little information and little interest in the specific grants managed by the governor's administration. As one deputy head of a midwestern health department noted in response to a question about legislative involvement in the grant process, "They can't go dollar by dollar through the hundreds of millions of dollars in grant aid we get."[48] Furthermore, there is no obvious reason why we should expect governors not to engage in what authors have called the "tactical distribution of grants,"[49] unless we assume that they do not wish to reward fellow partisans for loyalty, ensure the electoral success of legislators from the same party, and improve the overall fortunes of their party in the same way that presidents do.

Unfortunately, testing that expectation is far more difficult, from a data perspective, than examining the distribution of federal dollars by presidents. Some previous studies of the latter use the Federal Assistance Award Data System (FAADS) to directly track the transfer of federal resources to congressional districts.[50] Unfortunately, such a data source does not exist for state legislative districts. Alternatively, Larcinese and colleagues use the state year as the unit of analysis,[51] and in order to capture the degree of partisan agreement between members of Congress and the president, they measure the shared partisanship between the president and the majority of the state's congressional delegation. I use a similar strategy but focus on the county as the unit of analysis.

More specifically, I test whether counties receive more grant funding as the proportion of the state legislators from the governor's party representing some piece of the county increases. Data on total grants per capita for each county are drawn from the Consolidated Federal Funds Report and then married to the *State Legislative Election Returns, 1967–2003*, gathered by Carsey and colleagues in order to identify the legislator(s) that represent each county.[52] Combining these datasets is relatively time intensive because county identifiers are not included in the legislative elections data. Additionally, it is important to find states where counties, the unit at which one can measure grant allocation, and legislative districts, the unit at which one can measure partisanship, match as closely as possible. As a result, the analysis here is limited to counties in two states—Illinois and Kansas—for the five elections between 1994 and 2002.

Despite its small size, there are some characteristics of these states and years that make them attractive choices for this type of analysis. During the period under study, these states differed on most dimensions but were similar on one of theoretical interest. As such, they approximate a least similar systems design, which allows some cautious inference to other states. Between 1994 and 2002, one state had a Democratic and a Republican governor, while the other was led exclusively by Republicans. Additionally, whereas the Kansas legislature was controlled by the governor's party for the vast majority of the period under study, it was always controlled by the opposing party in Illinois. The Kansas governor has roughly the same formal powers as the average governor, whereas in Illinois the chief executive enjoys considerably more authority. Illinois is well above the national average in terms of urbanization and urban counties, while Kansas is a good deal more rural than the remainder of the nation. While Kansas was slightly below the national average in terms of personal income per capita, citizens in Illinois were better off relative to the mean.

One similarity that both Kansas and Illinois did share during this period, however, was the amount of grant funding coming into the state. Both states received less than the national average in inflation-adjusted per capita grant aid. Indeed, the totals received by each state during this period were statistically indistinguishable from one another. Additionally, the proportion of each state's grant funding made up by Medicaid, the largest formulaic federal program, was similar during this period. Illinois spent more total dollars on the program because of slightly higher benefit levels per beneficiary and slightly lower eligibility thresholds, but it was required to foot more of the bill with own-source funds than was Kansas, due to higher personal income levels. The results are similar if we look at the second-largest federal program—Highway Planning and Construction. Funding received from the Highway Trust Fund per dollar contributed by the state was comparable across the two states. While this book has made the argument that governors have significant influence over the expenditure of even formulaic grant funds through administrative decisions about the placement of state hospitals and clinics, the approval of transportation infrastructure projects, and so forth, similarities in the proportions of different types of grant funding between these states helps to ensure that those proportions are not driving the results.

The dependent variable in the model discussed below is the total inflation-adjusted grant aid per capita in each county and year. The variable is logged to make the distribution more normal and to reduce the influence of outliers such as Cook County in Illinois, which contains Chicago.

There are three independent variables and a set of interactive combinations of those variables in the model. The first is the proportion of the legislators from a county that are Democrats. This captures the fact that members of that party are more likely to represent urban counties and to have constituents that prefer a higher level of government service and are thus likely to receive higher levels of grant funding. The model also includes whether the governor is a Democrat, which is included in order to control for the possibility that that party might distribute more aid to all counties and, more importantly, to facilitate the inclusion of the key independent variable in the model. The final variable captures the competitiveness of elections in a county. Specifically, it is coded 1 if the majority of state legislative elections in districts that overlap the county were won by a vote margin of 10% or less. Higher competitiveness should lead to more grant funding, all else being equal, as governors and legislators have greater incentive to provide goods to voters. The key variables for hypothesis testing are the interactions, which include the interaction between the proportion of legislators that are Democrats and the party of the governor, as well as the three-way interaction between legislator partisanship, the party of the governor, and the competitiveness of races. If the two-way interaction is positive and significant, it will provide some support for the assertion that governors distribute more grant funding to copartisans in the legislature. If the three-way interaction is positive and significant, it will suggest that this effect is particularly large when legislators need grant aid in order to win.

Of course, the model includes a number of controls that may also influence the amount of grant funding received by a county. These include legislator characteristics, such as average time in office. I expect that longer-serving legislators will receive more funding, both because they have more experience securing funding for their districts and because they are more likely to occupy leadership positions, which gives them more to offer governors and agencies in return for funding. The model also includes a measure of population, which serves as another proxy for urbanization and captures the higher volume of grant aid available to such counties. Finally, the estimation includes year fixed effects in order to capture the different amount of grants available to or secured by states in different years and county fixed effects, which capture the influence of unmeasured variables on grant awards, including, for instance, whether the congressional representative is from the president's party.[53] The unit-level fixed effects also ensure that any observed relationships between gubernatorial party and grants are within rather than across counties. Finally, the model includes a dummy variable for Illinois.

The findings from the analysis of shared party and intrastate grant distribution are presented in table 4.3. The model performed very well, explaining 89% of the variation in the dependent variable. Population was positively correlated with grant expenditure. Both the year and the county fixed effects were jointly significant, suggesting that per capita awards to counties were in part a function of temporal changes and of unmeasured county-level variables.

Of course, the real variables of interest capture shared partisanship between legislators and the governor. First, we can observe that counties with a higher portion of Democratic legislators received more grant funding per capita, regardless of who controlled the governor's mansion. The coefficient suggests that a 1-standard deviation increase in the proportion of Democratic legislators within a county translates to 4.5% more grants, even when the governor is Republican. As noted above, this is probably a product of the type of counties in which Democrats are more likely to be elected. Competitiveness was positively correlated with grant awards to a county, which indicates that, all else being equal, governors were more likely to send grant money to places where additional public goods might help to secure electoral victory.

Table 4.3   Shared partisanship and grant disbursements to state legislators

Variables	Coefficients
Percentage democrat	.095*
	(.042)
Competitive	.131**
	(.038)
Democratic governor	−.263**
	(.085)
Percentage democrat × Democratic governor	.403*
	(.210)
Percentage Democrat × Democratic governor × competitiveness	−.178
	(.218)
Average years in office	−.006
	(.004)
Population	1.51e-06***
	(9.92e-08)
Illinois dummy	.824***
	(.072)

$N = 2064$
$R^2 = .89$
$F = 61.20$

Note: Model includes county and year fixed effects. Numbers in parentheses are standard errors.
*** $p<.001$, ** $p<.01$, * $p<.05$

The positive and significant two-way suggests that shared partisanship between the governor and a larger share of legislators dramatically increases grant distributions to a county. That coefficient, when combined with the one for main effect of legislator party, suggests that a 1-standard deviation increase in the percentage of Democratic legislators from a county is associated with a 19.5% increase in grants when the governor is a Democrat. The three-way interaction was not significant, indicating that the relationship between shared partisanship and allocations is not a function of the competitiveness of races within a county.

This result provides evidence for the assertion that governors spend grants strategically in order to help copartisans in the state legislature. They do not, however, support the electoral hypothesis, which would expect that the impact of shared partisanship would diminish in counties with more competitive races. Obviously, with this limited sample and time frame it is impossible to be certain that this result is not driven by congruence between the policy priorities of governors and the types of counties that copartisans represent.

However, given the magnitude of the impact and the presence of a control for gubernatorial party and county fixed effects, it is unlikely that the entire effect is due to this or some alternative cause. Nonetheless, the finding should be interpreted with caution and viewed primarily as a compliment to the other results in this chapter.

Conclusion

This chapter tests the book's general argument that governors use grants-in-aid to retain power for themselves or their parties by examining the expenditure of federal grants in the American states. It explores the degree to which grant funds are used to produce private benefits such as lower taxes as well as public goods in the form of increased state spending in targeted policy areas. It also investigates the ways in which governors claim credit for spending grants and the degree to which they use those funds to reward copartisans in the legislature. These tests provide remarkably consistent evidence that governors strategically use federal grants to produce policies preferred by core constituents. In every analysis discussed above, partisanship predicted grant-related behavior as expected. Republicans diverted more grant funds into lower taxes than did their Democratic counterparts, regardless of the method for calculating tax effort or the time period. Democrats spent more redistributive funds in targeted policy areas and claimed more credit for doing so, whereas distributive grants had a larger impact on own-source spending and received more attention in State of the State addresses under Republicans. Finally, members of both parties appear to send more federal funding to counties as the percentage of copartisans representing the area in the state legislature increases.

The results regarding opportunistic grant spending during election years are not as consistent, but they are still noteworthy. The analysis of the most updated measure of tax effort suggests that impending elections change the degree to which governors convert grants into lower taxes. The program-specific spending models also suggest that the stimulative effect of federal grants on state spending is also, at times, influenced by opportunistic behavior by governors facing reelection. Republican governors diverted more law enforcement and correction funding to other purposes when facing reelection—a choice likely counter to the preferences of their core constituents. Finally, there is some evidence that governors change the types of grants they claim credit for as elections approach—though, again, the finding is not as consistent as credit claiming targeted at core constituents.

It is important to remember that, as in the previous chapter, the results from these analyses arise from *within* state variation across time. In other words, what we are seeing is different grant expenditure patterns across parties and election cycles in each state, where presumably the other factors that might influence expenditure patterns are not as variable as they are across states. This empirical strategy allows for significantly greater confidence in the conclusion that observed grant expenditure patterns arise because governors are strategically using grants as a political resource.

Chapter Five

Grants and the Electoral Connection

In response to a deepening recession, Congress passed and President Obama signed the American Recovery and Reinvestment Act (ARRA) in 2009. Commonly referred to as the Stimulus Bill, the ARRA allocated $787 billion to be distributed to states and localities over ten years. The primary purposes of the funding were increasing economic growth and employment and revitalizing the nation's infrastructure.[1] The funds were distributed in the form of tax relief, grants, contracts and loans, and entitlement payments. While some states famously rejected small portions of Stimulus funding targeted at unemployment benefits, all governors accepted the lion's share of the federal funds initially offered to their states. Indeed, by the end of 2010, the federal government had distributed approximately $159 billion to state governments for the maintenance of social services and government jobs and to help recipients fill other gaps in their budgets. An additional $20 billion had been distributed for infrastructure maintenance and construction.[2]

The Stimulus represented an unprecedented short-term increase in federal dollars flowing into the states. In fact, ARRA money increased total federal funds received by the average state by almost 20% relative to 2009 levels. Any discussion of the "average" state, however, masks the significant interstate variation in the amount of Stimulus funding received in 2010. For example, while the mean value for that year was $761.05 per state resident, Alaska received more than $1,500 per capita. At the other end of the spectrum, Florida was awarded only $553 per resident in 2010. A host of factors were responsible for this state-to-state variation, but at least some of the differences were attributable to the actions of gubernatorial administrations, since initial awards were driven in part by the number of "shovel-ready" projects for which governors could claim there was an immediate need for funding in their states.

The Stimulus Bill was full of potential import because 37 governor's mansions were up for grabs the year that ARRA funds began arriving in the states. The evidence offered throughout this book, particularly from the analyses of State of the State speeches in the previous chapter, suggests that governors facing reelection probably tried to claim credit for this funding in order to enhance their probability of winning. Indeed, it is relatively easy to find examples of Stimulus-funded projects on the campaign trail. For example, Governor Martin O'Malley of Maryland, an incumbent Democrat with an approval rating of 48% visited Baltimore County in May 2010 to tout the $25-million Stimulus-funded replacement of a highway interchange. Similarly, Governor Jan Brewer of Arizona, a Republican with an approval rating of over 56%, made a stop at the University of Arizona's Science and Technology Park in July of that year to present $1.5 million in Stimulus money for the creation of a high-tech business incubator.

An initial look at the results of the 2010 gubernatorial contests also suggests that there may have been a connection between Stimulus funding and electoral success. States where the incumbent ran for reelection and won received $762.80 per capita from the ARRA in 2010. By contrast, the states where the incumbents lost their bids for reelection received only $620.14 per resident in Stimulus funding on average.

Of course, this simple correlation between federal money and election victories in the states does not demonstrate evidence for a consistent relationship between these variables over time. However, the result is consistent with the argument developed in chapter 2. The expectation that grant aid and electoral success may correlate arises from the antecedent argument that incumbents will use grant aid strategically to maximize approval among core constituents during most of their term and then, if necessary, to leverage support from noncore voters as elections approach. The preceding chapters have provided consistent evidence for these propositions—particularly for the use of grant aid by governors to pursue partisan goals. Governors are strategic actors who typically have at least a partial electoral motivation for their actions and possess limited time, energy, and money to achieve that goal. So the finding that they consistently use grants-in-aid for partisan and electoral purposes suggests they likely expect at least some electoral payoff from those activities.

This chapter is organized around testing the accuracy of that expectation. As in previous chapters, the empirical strategy will be to examine the relationship between grants and electoral success using multiple datasets, analytic techniques, and dependent variables. The first section offers the most direct test by exploring whether, between 1972 and 2004, incumbent governors who brought in more grant revenue were more likely to win reelection. The remaining sections explore the relationship between grants and some antecedents of electoral success. The first of these asks whether governors used grants to improve the public's assessment of their job performance from 1971 to 2005. The final section tests the degree to which grants correlate with gubernatorial success in the legislature.

Grants and Gubernatorial Elections

A large literature has examined the factors that influence the outcomes of gubernatorial elections in the American states.[3] Generally speaking this research has focused on the impacts of economic variables and noneconomic-issue voting.[4] Previous work in the latter area has found a link between electoral outcomes and crime, interest group endorsement, and abortion.[5] While these noneconomic studies are certainly important and insightful, work focused on the economic determinants of executive elections in the American states constitutes the largest portion of the literature. Because of the salience of the economy, studies of gubernatorial elections have long assumed that these contests are decided by retrospective economic voters.[6]

Interestingly, however, initial evidence regarding the effects of the economy on gubernatorial elections was actually quite mixed. Some of the earliest studies concluded that the economy, as measured through unemployment and inflation, was not an important determinant of electoral success.[7] However, studies that followed soon after, which examined larger samples of states and elections, found that voters penalized governors for increasing the state budget, while other factors outside the control of the governor, such as annual inflation rates, had little effect on gubernatorial elections. A related body of work on federalism and elections focused on the ability of voters to discern which level of government is most responsible for economic outcomes. Early research in this area generally found that governors are not punished for poor economic conditions because citizens held presidents and members of Congress responsible for the economy.[8]

More recent research on gubernatorial elections has found, however, that governors are held responsible for a poor state economy. It argues that the state's economy is a highly salient issue and that voters intuitively know how their state economy is performing relative to the national economy. For this reason, they argue that governors are ultimately responsible for the performance of the state economy and are often "visible targets of discontent" when a state performs poorly relative to the remainder of the nation.[9] Recent research has also found that incumbent governors are likely to be punished for increases in state taxes.[10]

The discrepancy between recent work, which finds that governors are held electorally responsible for state economies, and older work that found they were not, may be driven by institutional factors. In particular, authors have noted that most gubernatorial elections were shifted to non–presidential election years, which increased the likelihood that voters would blame state rather than national officials for current economic conditions. Additionally, as states' responsibility grew, the vast majority of governorships were expanded to four-year terms. This, along with the increased visibility of many governors during this period, also made it harder for them to avoid blame for the state's economy.[11]

Previous work on gubernatorial elections has not explored the impact of federal grants on the outcomes of those contests. This is unsurprising, given that previous work in fiscal federalism has not advanced the argument that grants might be used as political resources by electorally motivated incumbent governors. This book does offer that argument, suggesting that grants are a financial resource that governors may use to increase the chances that they, or someone from their party, will retain power. Grants make up roughly 20% of revenue in the average state, the largest category of revenues other than taxes. Earlier chapters provide considerable evidence that these monies are consistently spent to provide public and private goods preferred by core constituents and are sometimes spent opportunistically to capture a non-core median voter as elections approach. So, given the relative importance of grants to the average state economy and the evidence that governors spend those grants strategically, it seems reasonable that that the impact of these monies should be taken into account in studies of electoral success.

All else being equal, we can expect that governors who are able to dedicate more resources to the purposes of appealing to both core and noncore constituents should have more success getting reelected. Because governors from both parties appear to apply for and spend various grants for political purposes, the type of grant and the party of the incumbent receiving it should not be particularly important. Instead, the key variable should be *how much* grant funding an incumbent governor is successful in bringing into his or her state over the course of their term.

Of course, all incumbents do not run for reelection. In elections held between 1972 and 2004, an average of 20% of incumbents were prohibited from running for reelection due to term limits. Typically, in any given election during that period, another 25% chose not to run for some other reason. Even when they are not running for reelection, however, governors are acting as leaders of their party and are interested in maintaining the power of that party within the state. The literature on gubernatorial elections convincingly demonstrates that candidates from the same party as the sitting governor are rewarded or punished by voters for their actions.[12] Therefore, in addition to the expectation that grants should help incumbents get reelected, it is reasonable to assert that more grant aid will help the incumbent governor's party hold power, even if he or she does not run.

Finally, very recent work on policy shifts and electoral success can provide fine-grained expectations about the conditions under which governors should be able to use grants to increase the probability of reelection for themselves or their parties. That research theorizes that, when in power, parties adjust their policy priorities to match those of the public, conditional on the expected value of doing so. That literature defines "performance" as the accuracy with which a party adjusts its stated policy goals to match those of the public, given the strength of the public's desire for a policy and the risk of shifting government priorities. It finds that this measure of performance correlates with higher vote share for the incumbent party in the next election.[13]

Most importantly for the purposes of this discussion, Bertelli and John (2013) demonstrate that the relationship between policy representation and electoral success is moderated by the partisanship of the electorate. Specifi-cally, they show that positive impact of policy responsiveness *decreases* as par-tisan support for the prime minister's government increases. The explanation offered by the authors is quite intuitive: policy benefits "matter more when a larger compliment of swing voters is present" or, in other words, when the force of partisanship is weak enough to be overcome by those benefits.[14]

Based on this argument, I expect that the observed impact of grants will be larger when there is greater partisan division within a state. The logic underlying this expectation is very straightforward. When the median voter sits well within the bounds of the incumbent's core constituency, the policies that they are able to deliver via grant aid are likely to have little visible impact on elections because the electorate is already overwhelmingly predisposed to vote for the incumbent or his or her party. However, when the electorate is more closely divided, a governor may be able to sway those who lean toward his or her party with the provision of policies favored by the core and/or sway those that lean toward the opposition with opportunistic (i.e., noncore) poli-cies intended to appeal to those voters.

In keeping with most recent aggregate studies of gubernatorial elections, the dependent variable analyzed in this section is the vote share won by the incumbent's party.[15] The key independent variable captures the grant aid that a governor has brought into the state during her or his tenure. Specifically, the model includes the moving average of grant aid per capita for the election year and the three years prior. I believe that this measure of average aid over the course of the administration is preferable to one that reflects only election-year aid for two reasons. First, it is consistent with my assumption that grants can be used throughout an administration to reward core constituents as well as opportunistically as elections approach to woo swing voters. Second, the moving average measure helps control for the fact that, while grant aid to a state in any given year is in part a function of gubernatorial action, it also var-ies from year to year due to factors that are beyond the incumbent's control. The four-year moving average of grants is also logged to reduce the impact of significant outliers.

The second key independent variable is the interaction between the mov-ing average of grant awards and a measure of partisan heterogeneity. Specifi-cally, I interact grants with an index of partisan competition based on the per-centage of seats in the legislature controlled by each party. The competition variable is "folded" and scaled so that lower values represent greater partisan heterogeneity, while higher values show lower levels of partisan competition. In order to avoid omitted variables bias and ensure that the interaction can be interpreted correctly, the model also includes the measure of competition as a main effect.

The remaining variables in the model capture alternative explanations for incumbent party vote share. Probably most important among these is the electoral advantage that incumbents have in gubernatorial elections. Previous work consistently shows that the party in power can expect a large increase in vote share when the incumbent is in the race. Thus, the analysis includes an indicator coded 1 if the contest includes the incumbent, and 0 if the election is open.

Economic conditions constitute the next most frequently cited explanation for the outcomes in gubernatorial elections. In order to capture these, the model includes the difference between the state and national unemployment rates in the election year. Higher values suggest that the state is doing worse than the rest of the country, which should have negative electoral consequences for the incumbent governor or a candidate from his party. The model also includes the percentage of change in inflation-adjusted personal income per capita over the previous term. Positive values indicate that the average resident is doing better financially than when the current incumbent took office and should correlate positively with vote share. Finally, previous research suggests that incumbents and their parties may be penalized for increasing taxes.[16] Accordingly, the model includes an indicator of whether tax effort within a state went up during the current governor's administration.

Previous literature on gubernatorial elections has uncovered some evidence of a coattail effect in these contests, where a popular president can improve the fortunes of fellow partisans in the states. In order to capture this effect, the estimation discussed below includes a measure of the support for the president in the October Gallup poll of presidential approval. If the president is from the opposite party as the incumbent within a state, the inverse of the approval measure is used. Recent work has also emphasized the importance of campaign expenditures, both by incumbents and by their challengers, for the outcome of gubernatorial elections.[17] I capture this influence with measures of spending in the general and the primary election by the incumbent and his or her top three challengers in terms of spending.

These data are gathered from the Gubernatorial Campaign Finance Database created by Jensen and Beyle (2003).

Finally, recent scholarship has suggested that voters may hold incumbents accountable based on factors other than the economy. Specifically, a high crime rate is a salient issue that is likely to encourage retribution by voters. In order to control for this alternative issue, the model includes the crime rate within a state for each year collected from the Bureau of Justice Statistics. In a similar vein, it is reasonable to expect that incumbents in larger states will have more issues to deal with, and will thereby encounter more opportunities for electoral blame, than those in small homogeneous states. I control for this possibility by including the natural log of total state population in the model.[18]

The results from the analysis described above are presented in table 5.1. The model is estimated as a cross-sectional time-series, with state-election as the unit of analysis. The estimation includes state fixed effects, so the coefficients represent the impact of variables within states.

Looking first at the controls, we see that they perform largely as the existing literature suggests they should. Incumbents appear to enjoy a large advantage over challengers when running for reelection. At roughly 8%, this is the largest effect in the model. Similarly, and unsurprisingly, a recent tax increase has the opposite effect. There is significant evidence of a coattail effect, though the substantive impact of presidential popularity on vote share in gubernatorial contests is relatively small. Incumbent spending increases vote share, while spending by the challenger reduces the share won by the incumbent's party by a substantively important amount (marginal effect of 4%).

The main effect for partisan competition is *positive,* but it is important to remember that this counterintuitive coefficient represents the impact of that variable in a state that received no grant aid because of the interaction with that variable. It is therefore unrealistic. At the mean level of grant aid, an increase of 1-standard deviation in partisan competition *decreases* vote share by 3.4%.

Turning to the influence of grants, the variable measuring the moving average of total inflation adjusted grants-in-aid during a governor's term is positive and significant, suggesting that grants secured during an administration correlate positively with vote share for the incumbent's party in the current election. The interaction term between grants and partisan competition is

Table 5.1   The impact of grants on incumbent
party vote share in U.S. gubernatorial elections,
1972–2004

Variables	Coefficients
Grants	5.38*
	(2.79)
Competition	112.95*
	(63.38)
Grants × competition	−16.82[A]
	(10.04)
Relative unemployment	−0.98
	(1.19)
Change in personal income	0.15
	(0.11)
Tax increase	−2.29*
	(1.31)
Incumbent running	8.50***
	(1.19)
Presidential election year	1.55
	(2.86)
Presidential approval	0.02**
	(0.01)
Incumbent spending	7.32e-05*
	(3.8e-05)
Challenger spending	−8.6e-05***
	(2.2e-05)
Crime rate	−1.02e-3
	(1.28e-03)
Population	−2.79
	(6.75)

$N = 316$
$R^2 = .27$
$F = 7.37$

Note: Models include state fixed effects. Numbers in parentheses are standard errors ***$p<.01$, **$p<.05$, *$p<.1$,
[A]Jointly sig. $p<.1$

significant and negatively signed, which is consistent with the assertion that
the effect of grants should be reduced when the electorate is homogenously
supportive of the governor's party. The actual substantive impact of the interaction and the marginal effects of federal grants on vote share at different levels of partisan competition are presented graphically in figure 5.1. As the plot
indicates, the average level of federal funding secured throughout the course

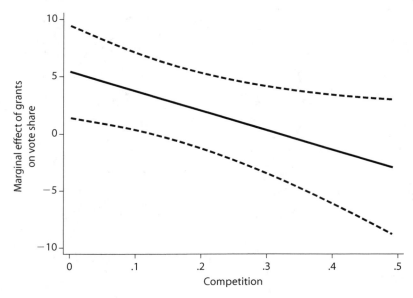

Figure 5.1 Impact of grants on incumbent party vote share at different values of party competition

of an administration has a marginal effect of 5% on expected incumbent party vote share when the legislature is essentially perfectly divided between Republicans and Democrats. This is the second-largest effect among all co-variates, behind only the bump experienced by incumbents actually seeking reelection. However, as competition decreases, so does the impact of grants. By the time it reaches slightly above the mean level, the effect of grants drops to 0. In other words, when the electorate is already fairly well aligned behind the party of the incumbent, more grants do not help him or her to buy a bigger portion of the vote.

Grants and Gubernatorial Approval

The results from the analysis discussed above support the expectation that governors who bring in more grant aid have greater electoral security, at least in those cases where that security might be in question due to heterogeneous preferences in the electorate. This is consistent with the argument that governors use grants as a political resource by delivering on campaign promises to core constituents and/or acting opportunistically to capture the median voter as elections approach. Obviously, however, these activities should also have an impact on some antecedents of reelection. If we can observe these relationships, it will bolster conclusions that there is truly a link between grants-in-aid and electoral success.

One of the most obvious antecedents to reelection is public approval.[19] The literature on gubernatorial approval has offered a number of insights into the determinants of a governor's popularity, though the findings from this work have, at times, been inconsistent. For example, numerous studies suggest that high unemployment lowers approval,[20] but others have found an inconsistent or no relationship between these variables.[21] Recent work has suggested that these inconsistencies might arise from the fact that gubernatorial popularity is a function of the state's unemployment rate *relative* to the national average, rather than simply the state's rate as measured in older work.[22] Similarly, there is somewhat mixed evidence that governors enjoy lower popularity under conditions of unified government—when they can easily be blamed for conditions within the state—and when they are governing a larger, more diverse state.[23] Previous work has also consistently found that governors are, not surprisingly, most popular immediately following their election and when they are of the same party as a popular president.[24]

The analysis in this section introduces grants-in-aid as a potential influence on gubernatorial popularity. Like the most recent work in this area, it makes use of the Official State Job Approval Ratings data to construct the dependent variable.[25] Unlike some of that work, which uses the individual poll as the unit of analysis, I aggregate to the state year. Doing so requires taking the mean value of available polls in those states and years where more than one poll was collected. More specifically, I use the average percentage of respondents giving a positive assessment of the governor's performance as the dependent variable.[26] The model is estimated as a cross-sectional time-series regression with state-level fixed effects, which help to isolate the impact of grants on approval *within* state and to control for unmeasured influences on the dependent variable. The model implements a correction for first-order auto correlation in order to deal with the fact that approval in year t is related to approval at t-1.

The key independent variable is the natural log of total inflation-adjusted federal grants per capita in each state and year. The control variables represent the explanations for gubernatorial approval offered in previous research. Specifically, the model includes a measure of the difference between the state unemployment rate and the national average. The model also includes the index of formal gubernatorial powers created by Beyle.[27] This variable captures, at least in part, the actual ability of the governor to influence state-level policies and outcomes that correlate with approval. The model also controls for the natural erosion of approval throughout a governor's term with an indicator coded 1 for the year immediately following an election, when approval should be highest. Previous research has suggested that it is difficult to maintain high approval ratings in larger, more diverse states, so the model also includes a measure of total population. In order to measure the influence of national politics, the analysis includes indicators of presidential election year, the president's approval rating, and whether or not the governor is from the same party as the president. Finally, the model controls for the party of the governor.

If the impact of grant aid on the electoral success of governors is moderated by partisan heterogeneity in the electorate, then the same might be true for approval. In other words, the degree to which an incumbent can influence his or her popularity via policies funded with federal grants could vary depending on the proportion of the electorate that is already predisposed to support or not support them. The theoretical support for this connection is more tenuous than for the connection between grants, partisan composition of voters, and electoral success because it is easy to imagine instances where someone might report support for an incumbent because of recent or salient events but support the other party in the next election. Nonetheless, it is important to control for the potential moderating impact of heterogeneity, and the model discussed below does so by including the interaction between grants and the index of partisan competition. In order to allow for an accurate interpretation of the interaction, the model also includes the competition variable as a main effect. The results from the analysis of gubernatorial approval are presented in table 5.2.

For the most part, the controls in this analysis perform largely as expected, with approval going up early in the governor's term and down when the state unemployment rate is higher than the national average. Of course, the coefficient of interest here is the one for federal grants. It is positive and significant, suggesting that an increase in federal grants is associated with an increase in gubernatorial popularity. The interaction between grants and competition is also statistically significant and negative, indicating that the relationship between grants and approval is moderated by partisan heterogeneity. A plot

Table 5.2   The impact of grants on gubernatorial approval, 1971–2005

Variables	Coefficients
Grants	11.43***
	(1.93)
Competition	178.24
	(109.09)
Grants × competition	−27.21*
	(16.12)
Republican governor	0.91
	(1.37)
Formal powers	−3.84
	(3.35)
Honeymoon	1.41*
	(0.86)
Relative unemployment	−2.36**
	(0.81)
Presidential election year	0.68
	(0.75)
Population	−2.52e-06
	(1.54e-06)

$N = 594$
$R^2 = .15$
$F = 10.34$
rho = .64

Note: Models include state fixed effects. Numbers in parentheses are standard errors *** $p<.01$, ** $p<.05$, * $p<.1$

of marginal effects (figure 5.2) suggests that grants have an effect of as much as 11% on a governor's approval rating when political competition is highest. The effect diminishes as the state becomes more homogenous politically but persists in approximately 90% of states.[28]

To give an idea of what these results mean substantively, consider the following. It easy to find examples, including the administrations of Bill Owens (R-CO), Jane Hull (R-AZ), and numerous others, where governors increased funding by ½-sd in a single term. Given the level of competition in each of these states, the results presented in table 5.2 suggest that these governors would have been able to use grants-in-aid to produce a 3 to 4% bump in their approval ratings. Given all of the other factors that influence an executive's popularity as well as the scrutiny under which most modern governors oper-

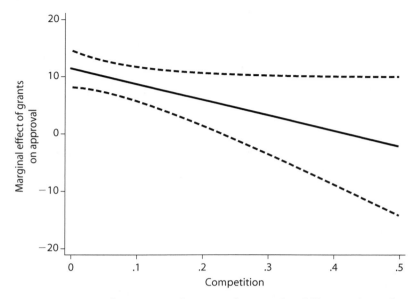

Figure 5.2 Impact of grants on gubernatorial approval at different values of party competition

ate, this is a very large impact. Additionally, because of the well-established relationship between approval and electoral success, the association between grants and approval helps confirm the veracity of the finding regarding the electoral payoff of grants-in-aid reported in the previous section.

Grants and Legislative Success

There are, of course, other important antecedents of electoral success that we might expect to correlate with grants-in-aid. Research at the federal level suggests that legislative success is one such precursor of electoral fortune. As King notes, "All you [the president] really need from Congress is votes, but you need those votes really badly. . . . You need those votes to enable you to build up a record, to win reelection, to win—who knows?—a place in history."[29] Most germane to this argument, scholars have suggested that presidents may use grants in order to help secure those votes.

It is reasonable to expect that governors have a similar need to secure votes from their colleagues in the legislature. Indeed, Kousser and Phillips (2012) state it quite clearly: "Voters demand policy leadership and results from the governors whom they send to office." Their work also highlights the significant institutional and constitutional obstacles that governors face when trying to fulfill those expectations as well as the tremendous effort they expend in attempting to surmount them. Ultimately, the authors conclude that governors are "powerful players" in the formulation of public policies (winning some type of legislative support almost 60% of the time) and in the budget process (getting almost 70 cents in the final budget deal for every dollar change they propose).[30]

Kousser and Phillips's conclusions accord relatively well with the results of previous work. Authors have long supposed that governors, because of their role as chief legislators and their high profile in state government, have significant power in the policymaking process.[31] Empirical studies of *generalized* gubernatorial influence on policy—often testing hypothesized relationships between Democrats and redistributive policy—have arrived at mixed conclusions.[32] However, work that looks directly for a relationship between a governor's policy *priorities* and legislative success on related bills has typically concluded that governors do enjoy some success shepherding their agendas through the legislative process.[33]

Of course, this work has identified a set of factors that condition gubernatorial success in the legislature, including the time left in their terms, the economic conditions within a state, and the party that controls the legislature, among others. Kousser and Phillips's game theoretic models of influence predict (somewhat intuitively) that governors with the most powerful rewards and punishments to offer legislators and who wish to move the status quo in the same direction as the legislative majority will have greater success. In terms of the inducements that a governor might offer legislators, they suggest: "Lawmakers who work toward the passage of the executive agenda can expect to receive favors such as support for their reelection campaigns and fund-raising efforts, plumb appointments for their political allies, and joint appearances with the governor in their districts. The governor can also transform her veto authority from a negative to a positive power by promising to sign bills that are important to individual lawmakers in exchange for their support of her proposals."[34]

To date, however, no study of gubernatorial success, including Kousser and Phillips's has considered the degree to which governors might use grants-in-aid to improve the fortunes of their agendas in the legislature. Given the evidence that presidents use grants in just this way, along with the findings from the previous chapters that governors pursue and spend grant aid strategically and distribute more grant aid to co-partisans, it seems reasonable to expect that such a correlation might exist. The remainder of this section specifies a model that tests for a correlation between federal grants available to governors and their degree of legislative success.

My strategy for this analysis is to analyze a validated measure of gubernatorial success rather than try to create a new one. Though there are other alternatives, the analysis here uses a measure created by Kousser and Phillips for a variety of reasons.[35] First, it is the most recent, examining legislative success by U.S. governors in 2001.[36] Second, it has high face and construct validity because the authors use State of the State speeches to identify gubernatorial priorities and then consult external sources to validate the issues and items identified. Finally, Kousser and Phillips offer a measure of success weighted by the significance of the victory and broken down by issue area (budget vs. other policy), which other studies do not.

These final distinctions are quite important for the purposes of this project. The argument here is that governors can use grants to increase legislative success, which in turn leads to greater electoral security for themselves and their parties. If that is indeed the case, then it is reasonable to expect a relationship between available grant aid and *meaningful* pieces of legislation, because these are the ones that create a policy record that incumbents can sell to voters. The Kousser and Phillips measure allows us to observe this type of success by weighing each case of gubernatorial "success" by several relevant factors. According to the authors, the "scores give governors points for each of their accomplishments, with more points assigned when they win bigger and more complete victories."[37]

Additionally, the Kousser and Phillips measure allows us to discern if grants-in-aid have a differential impact on gubernatorial success in budget versus policy-related bills, which the authors suggest pose distinct challenges for governors. A relationship between grants and success in either area will help to bolster confidence in the observed relationship between grants and electoral security, because incumbents could run on either their victories regarding spending or their policy. An association between grant aid and success in both areas will do even more to confirm the assertion that there is a connection between grants and electoral security.

Despite their advantages for this analysis, the most obvious shortcoming of the Kousser and Phillips impact scores is that they are available for only

27 states. Because of the limited sample of both states and the cross-sectional design necessitated by the measures, the results discussed below should be interpreted with a good deal of caution.

The key independent variable in my analysis is the total amount of grant aid available to a governor. The model actually includes the natural log of total grant aid per capita in order to account for the large variation in population and grant aid received across the small sample of states for which the dependent variable is available.[38]

The control variables in the analysis are similar to those in previous studies of legislative success. The model includes a measure of the Beyle index of the governor's formal powers, based on the assumption that governors with a higher score will have greater influence on the legislature through their agenda setting, budgetary, and veto powers. It also includes the Squire index of legislative professionalism in order to account for the likelihood that governors will have different levels of success depending on the resources and expertise available to legislators.[39] The analysis includes an indicator coded 1 if it is the year following the governor's election, in order to account for higher levels of success observed during this "honeymoon" period. The model controls for total population in order to capture the challenges that governors might face in a legislature that represents a larger and/or more diverse population. It also includes a measure of per capita income. Finally, the model controls for the party of the governor and the presence of unified government. The literature does not suggest a clear expectation regarding gubernatorial party, but it does suggest that governors consistently win more and bigger victories when facing a legislature controlled by their party.[40]

The results from the analyses discussed above are presented in table 5.3. The first model presents the impact score for budget-related bills, the second presents the policy-related score, and the final column contains results from the model of the total impact score. The models are estimated as ordinary least squares regressions and report robust standard errors.

Before looking at the impact of grants, it is interesting to examine the controls, which tend to perform relatively differently across the various scores. For example, the formal powers of the governor are positively correlated with success on policy-related bills and on the overall impact score, but they do not appear to help a governor win budget battles. The findings for the party of the governor suggest a similar pattern. Alternatively, unified government is positively associated with budgetary impact and the total score but not

Table 5.3   The impact of grants on legislative success by governors, 2001

Variables	Budget bills	Policies	Total impact
Grants	5.48*	6.87[A]	12.35**
	(2.86)	(4.45)	(4.91)
Republican	0.12	11.73**	11.85**
	(2.88)	(3.98)	(5.26)
Formal powers	−2.02	14.69***	12.45*
	(5.18)	(4.01)	(6.91)
Honeymoon	−0.51	4.25	3.74
	(3.01)	(3.75)	(5.54)
Unified government	4.94*	4.48	9.43*
	(2.89)	(4.30)	(5.50)
Legislative professionalism	−11.69	19.27[A]	7.58
	(9.43)	(11.85)	(13.05)
Per capita income	−1.42e-04	−8.12e-04**	−6.70e-04
	(2.15e-04)	(3.98e-04)	(4.78e-04)
$N =$	27	27	27
$R^2 =$	0.26	0.47	0.39
$F =$	1.44	4.1	2.13

Note: Numbers in parentheses are robust standard errors. ***$p<.01$, **$p<.05$, *$p<.1$, [A]$p<.1$ (one-tailed test)

with success on other important policy initiatives. Finally, the results suggest that governors have more success on major policy bills when facing legislatures with a higher degree of professionalism, but the Squire measure is not significantly related to overall success or success on budget bills. These inconsistent results actually accord quite well with Kousser and Phillips's assertion that governors face different constraints and enjoy different levels of success depending on whether they are bargaining with the legislature over budgets or policy.

Interestingly, the models in table 5.3 suggest that the same cannot be said about the impact of grants. As the table suggests, logged grants per capita have a positive and significant relationship with the impact scores for budget bills, other types of policies, and all bills combined. In terms of the substantive impacts, the coefficient for grants in the first column suggests that a change from the minimum to the maximum grant amount correlates with approximately a 1-sd increase in major or complete victories on budgetary matters. The impact on non-budgetary policy matters is somewhat smaller, with the coefficient in column 2 suggesting a ½-sd change in impact across

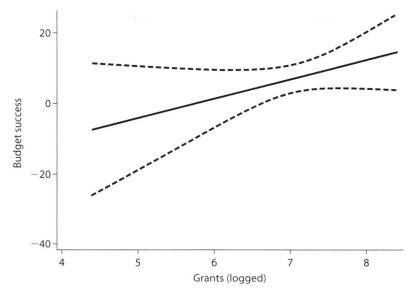

Figure 5.3 Impact of grants on gubernatorial budget success in the legislature

the range of the grant measure. Finally, the results suggest that the impact of grants grows again in the model of total impact to approximately a 1-sd change in success across the range of the grants measure.

These effects are perhaps easier to comprehend graphically. Figures 5.3 to 5.5 graph the predicted value of budgetary, policy, and total legislative success across the range of the grants measure.[41] As the figures suggest, very low levels of grants are not significantly associated with success. However, at higher levels grant totals become positively associated with more success. Specifically, the results suggest that governors are likely to secure victory on about 20 additional significant budget requests if they bring in the maximum versus the mean amount of federal grant aid. The size of the impact is similar in the case of total major gubernatorial priorities realized and slightly smaller in the case of policy-specific victories.

The substantive importance of these results is bolstered by an assessment of the impact of grants relative to other variables in the models. In the analysis of total impact score, the size of the effect for grants is statistically indistinguishable from those for unified government and the formal powers of the governor. In the model budgetary bills, the effect is statistically indistinguish-

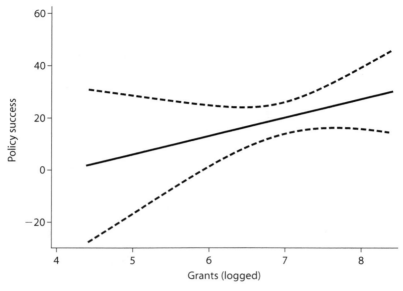

Figure 5.4 Impact of grants on gubernatorial policy success in the legislature

able from that of the only other significant predictor—unified government. The effect of grants fares somewhat worse, relative to other predictors at least, in the model of non-budgetary policy impact. In that analysis, it is statistically equivalent to the effect for professionalism but significantly smaller than the impact of gubernatorial party, personal income, and gubernatorial powers. It is interesting to note, however, that grants do have between 30 and 50% as large an impact as these other variables and are thus far from trivial.

Conclusion

This chapter began with an anecdote suggesting that governors may have benefited electorally from the active pursuit of Stimulus funding during the Great Recession. The examples offered there, while admittedly cherry-picked, are a perfect microcosm of the larger argument that governors strategically pursue and spend federal grants in an attempt to increase electoral security for themselves and their parties. The chapter has sought to provide more compelling evidence for that argument and to demonstrate that governors do indeed benefit electorally from grants-in-aid.

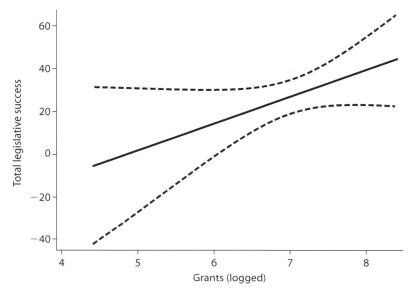

Figure 5.5 Impact of grants on total gubernatorial success in the legislature

The results of the three analyses provide that evidence, while illuminating the conditions under which grants are likely to have the biggest impact on electoral success. The average total grant aid that incumbents are able to bring in over the course of their administration correlates positively with the vote share won by their party in the next election. As expected, the relationship between grants and electoral success is only significant in the presence of partisan diversity within the electorate. In other words, grants do not make a meaningful difference when a state's population is already firmly aligned behind one party. When they are on the fence, however, and partisan loyalties are divided, grants can influence vote margin by enough to swing a tightly contested election.

Obviously, there are a lot of intervening factors that might help link available grant resources to electoral outcomes, and uncovering a relationship between grants and these factors should bolster our confidence in the main result. This chapter has focused on two of these factors, gubernatorial approval and legislative success. In both cases, analyses have suggested that grants-in-aid correlate positively with important antecedents of electoral success.

Chapter Six

Conclusion

Grants-in-aid have arguably been the dominant tool with which the national government has pursued its policy priorities in the U.S. federal system for almost five decades. Except for a brief hiatus in the 1980s, federal transfers to state and local governments as a percentage of gross domestic product have trended steadily upward during that period. The proposed budget for FY2012 included more than $583 billion in grant funding spread across more than 1,000 programs. In the average state, federal grants made up 24% of total revenue in 2009, which was the second-largest category of revenue behind taxes and was actually larger than any *individual* category of tax revenue (i.e., income, sales, etc.). This has led some observers to suggest that state dependence on federal funds has effectively allowed the national government to preempt policy-making authority in most issue areas.[1]

Despite its prevalence, however, that story of subnational dependence often does not match the actual behavior of state governments. Indeed, this book opened with the decision made by many states to forgo *billions* of dollars in federal funds available for expanding Medicaid coverage under the

Affordable Care Act. Medicaid expansion was by no means the only recent example of states refusing to accept large federal grants or even returning already-allocated funds. In 2010, seven governors rejected their states' portion of roughly $7 billion in Stimulus money designed primarily to extend unemployment benefits to part-time workers.[2] In that same year, Governor Rick Scott (R-FL) rejected the previously approved plans for a high-speed rail line between Orlando and Tampa, and in doing so turned down almost $2 billion in federal grant funds. In 2011, Governor Sam Brownback (R-KS) refused a $31.5 million grant that his state had been awarded by the Department of Health and Human Services for being an "early innovator" in the creation of the health insurance exchanges mandated by the Patient Protection and Affordable Care Act. Numerous other states rejected smaller planning grants intended to facilitate the creation of exchanges or, in one case, accepted the money and then simply refused to begin developing an exchange.[3] In other words, the story is considerably more complex than one of national government hegemony.

The obvious conclusion is that "politics" played a large role in these decisions to push back against the power of the federal purse. After all, the governors that chose to reject unemployment, high-speed rail, and ACA grants offered by the Obama administration were all Republicans, as were the vast majority of those that chose not to expand Medicaid. Again, however, the real story may be more nuanced than a simple tale of national partisan priorities driving state behavior. We've long assumed that politicians are strategic in pursuit of policy and political goals, which would imply that decisions by governors to leave huge sums of federal money on the table were purposive and goal driven. This appears even more likely when we dig a little deeper and examine the cases in which governors chose to *accept* or even *pursue* grants that the majority of their colleagues were loudly rejecting. To revisit an example from chapter 1, the Republican governors that agreed to the eligibility changes necessary to assure their share of Medicaid expansion dollars faced significantly more liberal constituencies and lower electoral security than did their counterparts in other states. The same can be said of many of the Republicans that accepted high-speed rail funds and produced high-quality applications for Race to the Top funds.

Thus, it would appear that recent grant-related decision making in the states was not driven by dependence and was more than a simple knee-jerk rejection of Democratic programs by members the opposing party. The problem is that existing theories offer very little insight into the politics of grant-related decision making in the states and even less into the seemingly strategic use of federal grants by state-level politicians. That gap between observed behavior and social scientific explanations for it provided the impetus for this book. The remainder of this concluding chapter will briefly review the theoretical perspective that guided the inquiry as well as the major finding that it produced. It will also draw out the implications of those results for some of the major issues in the study of federalism, including the safeguards of state authority in federal systems, the impact of federal grants on state policy priorities, and the influence of federalism on state elections.

Theoretical Argument and Major Findings

The theoretical approach that motivates analyses throughout this book is very straightforward. It argues that state-level politicians have significant electoral incentives to manipulate the grant-in-aid system to their advantage and suggests that, because of their influence over executive agencies and the budget process, governors are particularly well positioned to do so. Asserting that the handling of grants-in-aid is closely analogous to other spending decisions, it draws on the literature in comparative political economy in order to develop specific expectations about the strategic use of federal grants by incumbent governors. The theory produces a set of three interrelated hypotheses. The first is that incumbents will pursue and spend grants in an effort to increase electoral security by delivering policies desired by core constituents. Second, it also suggests, however, that when electoral security is low, incumbents may use grants opportunistically to fund public and private goods that appeal to a noncore median voter. Finally, the theory produces the expectation that, because of the strategic use of federal money by incumbents, grants-in-aid help governors to improve their popularity and secure reelection.

Analyses of more than three decades of data on the receipt and expenditure of grants in all 50 states as well as interviews with state officials and assessments of governors' public speeches provides strong support for the assertion that governors strategically use grants as an electoral resource. The most common way in which they do so is by pursuing and spending grants that provide goods and services desired by core constituents. The evidence for this behavior is remarkably consistent, appearing in 16 different analyses throughout this book. Those analyses suggest that states increase their participation in redistributive versus social regulatory grant programs when a Democrat replaces a Republican in the governor's mansion and that Democrats within a state receive more money from regulatory and redistributive programming, while their Republican counterparts get more federal money targeted at social regulation and economic development. The analyses here also show that Republican governors are less likely to apply aggressively for a competitive grant focused heavily on educational inequality and that they are more likely to apply for and use 1115 and 1915 waivers to repurpose federal social welfare funds flowing into their states.

In addition to pursuing different grants, the evidence demonstrates quite clearly that governors from opposing parties spend federal monies differently and in a way that is consistent with the preferences of their respective core constituents. Republican governors are more likely divert a higher proportion of grant aid to private benefits, such as lower taxes, preferred by their base. Redistributive grants, such as Medicaid, have a larger stimulative effect on state spending under Democratic governors, while in the same state more state money "sticks" to distributive and social regulatory grants when a Republican is in the governor's mansion. An examination of State of the State speeches reveals that governors want constituents to know about these decisions. Thus, Republicans are more likely to claim credit for highway expenditure, veterans benefits, spending on law enforcement, and economic development activities; while Democrats are significantly more likely to tout the use of grants for expanding health care coverage, increasing educational access or quality for low-income children, and increasing environmental regulation. Finally, there is evidence that state agencies spend more federal grant money in counties represented more heavily in the state legislature by members of the governor's party. Taken together, these results provide remarkable evidence that, all else being equal, governors spend grants-in-aid strategically in order to maximize the production of goods and services desired by core constituents.

The evidence that governors adapt their grant-related behavior when electoral security is low is more mixed. Nonetheless, there are plenty of instances throughout the book where, as elections approach, incumbents begin to pursue and spend grants for purposes likely to appeal to members of the *other* party. It is reasonable to conclude, therefore, that governors sometimes strategically use grants-in-aid in order to capture a median voter who may sit outside of their core constituency. For example, in most of the project grants examined, the receipt of funds from programs favored by the governor's base went *down* in election, as compared to nonelection, years.[4] Similarly, Republican governors were more aggressive in applying for President Obama's Race to the Top competition if they were running for reelection. Finally, Republicans were more likely than Democrats to seek waivers to impose work requirements and time limits on AFDC recipients during nonelection years, but those differences disappeared when the incumbent was seeking reelection.

More examples of adaptation of grant-related behavior during times of electoral insecurity emerged from the analyses of grant expenditure. In the analysis utilizing the most recently developed measure, Democrats diverted less grant money into lower tax effort than did Republicans in the same state, but the difference between the parties disappeared in election years. Models of specific grants showed that federal law enforcement and corrections grants had a much larger stimulative effect when received by Republican governors who were not running for reelection compared to those facing an election. Finally, analyses of governor's State of the State speeches suggest that Republicans actually spend a *higher* proportion of their speech claiming credit for redistributive spending than do Democrats during election years, which represents a reversal of the pattern observed during years without an election.

So, while it is not as robust as the finding of partisan effects, evidence is still substantial that governors strategically use grants to appease *noncore* voters during election years. The relative strength of these results accords well with the larger literature on political spending cycles, where authors have had a considerably easier time finding partisan versus electoral effects. For the purposes of this book, however, the results regarding the partisan pursuit and expenditure of federal grants as well as that regarding the moderating effect that electoral security has on that relationship are more than sufficient to conclude that governors are using grants-in-aid strategically as a political resource.

There is also clear evidence that incumbents can convert that resource into electoral security. Chapter 5 demonstrates that grants-in-aid help governors maintain higher approval ratings, achieve passage of their legislative agenda, and ultimately retain the governor's mansion for themselves or members of their party. It is important to note, however, that the impact of grants on electoral fortune is conditional on the degree of partisan division within the state. The political resource that grants represent does not make a meaningful difference when a state's population is already firmly aligned behind one party. However, when partisan loyalties are divided, strategic use of grants-in-aid can influence vote margin by enough to secure victory for incumbents and their party.

Implications

These results have a number of significant implications for the study of federalism and state politics. First, the finding that governors strategically use grants-in-aid as a political resource suggests a hitherto unexplored influence on state-level elections. The large and rich literature on gubernatorial elections has focused heavily on the impact that economic conditions and tax burden play in those contests. To date, federalism has played a relatively tangential role in the story, serving primarily as a way for scholars to test whether voters could accurately assign credit or blame for unemployment and tax increases to state and national politicians.

The analyses contained here suggest another, much more direct impact of federalism on state elections. The average margin of victory in gubernatorial contests over the past century or so is a whopping 21%. When you take out the pre–Voting Rights Act South, however, that number drops substantially, because states like South Carolina and Georgia, where victorious candidates regularly won by more than 70 points, tend to skew the mean. Even including those states and that time period in the sample, however, roughly 60% of governor's races over the last century have been won by less than a 10% margin of victory.[5] More than a third of the gubernatorial contests in 2012 were decided by five points or less.

All of this is relevant because grants-in-aid secured during a governor's administration can move vote share by more than 5% under the right circumstances.[6] In other words, grants can make a big enough difference in vote share to swing a nontrivial percentage of elections to the incumbent or a member of her party. So, rather than an indirect coattails or attribution error effect on gubernatorial elections, federalism may have a direct and meaningful impact on the outcome of contests because governors are able to strategically use federal grants as an electoral resource. Of course, it is important to remember that the impact of grants on vote share has a lot to do with the level of partisan division within a state and that the effect is visible only in states with relatively high levels of political competition. However, the moderating impact of competition makes the implications of grants for gubernatorial elections *even greater* because it is in competitive states where margins of victory are often smallest.

Though there are obviously numerous other factors that influence the fortunes of political parties in elections for governor, the predicted effects of grants offered here fit well with general trends in grant receipt and electoral success over the past 50 years. Prior to 1984, Democratic governors brought in significantly more grant aid per capita than their Republican counterparts, particularly in competitive states. During that same period, the Democratic Party controlled 62% of governor's mansions. By the late 1980s, however, the difference between grants per capita in Republican- and Democrat-controlled states had become statistically indistinguishable from 0. Between 1996 and 2005, when Republicans held 57% of governorships, members of that party were bringing in a significantly higher amount of grant aid per resident relative to Democrats. Again, the differences were even larger in competitive states, where the findings from this analysis suggest it should have mattered most.

It is also possible that the impacts of grants-in-aid on state elections reported in this book are underestimated on at least one dimension. The analyses demonstrate that grants are used strategically and that they correlate with electoral fortune. They do not, however, explicitly model the fact that some governors are likely more adept than others at converting grant funding into vote share. In cases where governors are highly skilled at choosing and applying for grant programs and at deciding which constituents to target with those funds, the impact of fiscal federalism on electoral outcomes could be significantly greater than suggested here. Future work will explore the accuracy of the strategic decisions governors make about federal grants, the factors that predict better and worse use of grants as a political resource, and the impact that such variation has on the relationship between grants and electoral success for incumbents and their parties.

The second important implication of the results from this project speaks to the persistent question of grant effectiveness. For more than half a century scholars have debated the degree to which federal grants stimulate state-level spending in targeted policy areas. Conclusions regarding the flypaper effect—or the degree to which state money "sticks" to federal money—vary widely depending on the time period, program, study methodology, and numerous other factors. Nonetheless, essentially every study finds that states substitute at least some federal money for own-source funds that would have otherwise been spent in a particular area.

Grant effectiveness (or lack thereof) is more than just an intellectual curiosity and has real implications for the effectiveness of central governments in dealing with the policy problems that often arise in federal systems. Federations of autonomous governments are significantly more susceptible than other forms to spillover effects, where the action or inaction of one government influences the well-being of others and the whole. Grants-in-aid are one of the primary tools by which central governments mitigate negative spillovers. Major grant programs throughout U.S. history have been targeted at ameliorating poor health, limited education, poverty, and other issues that, while historically the purview of individual state governments, have the potential to damage the Union as a whole if left unchecked. For the most part, grants-in-aid do not serve this purpose as effectively if they are being treated as income by recipient governments. In other words, there may not be sufficient resources to address spillovers if state governments supplant rather than supplement their own spending with federal grants-in-aid.

Predictions regarding, and proposals for mitigating, the degree of grant fungibility have been heavily focused on the behavior of the federal government. Matching requirements, maintenance of effort (MOE) stipulations, and the careful monitoring of grantees have long been suggested as the best means for reducing the substitution of federal grants for state funds; however, as noted in various places throughout this book, the effectiveness of these tools is questionable at best. Another, far more limited line of work has suggested that the policy preferences of grantees is a good place to start if you want to understand how they spend grant money. The results from this project speak directly to this debate and significantly expand our understanding of grant effectiveness in a couple of ways.

First, the findings suggest that grants are most effective when they increase the electoral security of state-level incumbents. When elections are still a long way off (at least in political terms), that security is driven by appeals to the base; so regardless of grant type, matching and MOE requirements, or program salience, grants that fund public goods preferred by a governor's core constituents are going to stimulate more state spending on targeted public goods. This makes them, at least from the vantage of a federal government trying to increase production of those goods, a better investment. From that perspective, grants awarded to Democrats are also a better investment because, all else being equal, Republicans are more likely to appeal to their base by using federal funds to maintain or lower tax rates.

The results also suggest, however, that federal actors interested in the impact of grants-in-aid must be cognizant of election timing in the states. During election years, when electoral security is necessarily lower, incumbents are more likely to spend federal money in a way that benefits the median voter, regardless of their partisan preferences. On the one hand, for grants that are already stimulating spending in targeted areas this is bad news, because it suggests that sometime within the next four years that effect may be diluted by electoral pressures. Alternatively, it also suggests a moment when the national representativeness of grant expenditures may be at its highest. In those years when 36 governor's mansions from all quarters of the country are up for grabs, the preferences of those state-level median voters are likely to aggregate fairly closely to the national median. If the national government is using grants to pursue policies that appeal to that voter, then these mega-gubernatorial election years are the period when grant aid is most likely to produce public goods that are representative of the citizenry as a whole. That, in and of itself, might be construed as a type of effectiveness.

With all that said, the second thing that the analyses throughout the book suggests about grant effectiveness is that grants-in-aid are a relatively *ineffective* tool of federal policy making. More importantly, they suggest that it will be very difficult to make them otherwise. If we return to the traditional definition of effectiveness as the ability to move recipient spending or policy in a direction preferred by the grantor, the results here consistently show that such a standard is only partially met at best. This is not the first time this has been argued, of course.

What this study does contribute, however, is a better understanding of the reasons for that failure. If grant expenditure is driven by fiscal need within a state or ideological attachment to certain programs, then matching requirements and monitoring may serve to discourage diversion of funds away from targeted areas. Grant expenditure appears, however, to be driven by something much more fundamental—political survival. If we believe the mountain of evidence suggesting that reelection is one of, if not *the* primary motivation of incumbent politicians, then it is difficult to imagine a federal incentive robust enough to keep state-level politicians from using grants as a resource in pursuit of that goal.

This discussion of the relative effectiveness of grants as a federal policy tool brings us to a third and final implication suggested by this book. Scholars and pundits have long debated Madison's notion that there are inherent protections of state authority built into the U.S. political system. Many now explicitly reject the notion of political safeguards, arguing that any protections that once existed have long since been demolished. These claims often rest primarily on evidence of the dramatic increase in national government preemptions and mandates over the course of the twentieth century, but some have also suggested that grants-in-aid help to erode state power in the federal system. The argument is that the proliferation of federal money; the coupling of aid to programs (like Medicaid), which the states cannot do without and cannot fund themselves; and the devolution of policy responsibility by the national government have combined to create a high level of fiscal dependence among the states. This dependence, in turn, allows the federal government to "preempt" state policy-making decisions via the conditions associated with grants.

The analyses presented throughout this book cannot speak to the relationship between tools like preemption and state sovereignty, but they do provide considerable evidence that grants are not a threat to state prerogatives. The discretion that state actors exercise in the pursuit and expenditure of grants-in-aid makes them much more of a cooperative rather than a coercive policy tool. In other words, in spite of the many conditions attached to them, federal funds seem to help states pursue the policy priorities of their governors rather than coerce them into adopting the policy priorities of the federal government.

There are clearly incentives for states to move toward federal priorities inherent in the grant system, but these are far from the hegemonic source of policy influence that some would suggest. As one director of a midwestern education agency put it, "Generally, we go after two kinds of grants—things that give us an avenue for other funding and things that the federal government makes really attractive because they are trying to get states to move into an area that they consider a priority." In response to a follow-up question about what they meant by "other funding," the respondent said, "You know, we look at grants that tie into the services we are already funding." The importance of state priorities in grant-related decisions is even more visible in the response of an education official from the Northwest who, when asked if the governor played a role in deciding which grants they applied for, replied, "Absolutely. The governor is required to sign off, at least on major initiatives, so I don't see how it could be any other way."

Though it was more difficult to get state officials to speak openly about it, it is equally clear from the numerous statistical analyses that state priorities play a significant role in decisions about how grant monies are spent. The correlation between the preferences of governors and grant expenditure persisted even in programs where grant design and monitoring should have safeguarded federal interests in spending decisions. In the presence of such discretion regarding both the receipt and expenditure of federal funds, it is difficult to argue that grants serve as an effective tool of policy centralization in the United States.

Indeed, the pervasive evidence of state priorities in fiscal federalism relationships might lead one to argue that grants actually constitute a *safeguard* of federalism. One of the key reasons that decentralized arrangements like federalism work is that they can tolerate a diversity of preferences or, more specifically, allow for the policy variation necessary to maintain the support of a large and homogenous population.[7] Across every policy area, states are able to use the grants-in-aid system to provide more of the public goods and services their citizens prefer, to maintain the balance between benefits and taxation demanded by those citizens, and even to experiment with and adapt national programs in a way that makes them palatable to local preferences. In other words, grants facilitate the state-level variation in policy attributed to federalism.

If we were willing to assume that it had perfect information, which of course it does not, and no moral hazard problem, which of course it has, the federal government might be able to limit this function for grants and make them more a tool of centralization. Despite decades of strong and consistent evidence that states adapt grants to their purposes, however, national actors have proven themselves unwilling to curtail that discretion. Over the years, the Office of Management and Budget (OMB) and the Government Accounting Office (GAO) have provided the president and members of Congress with dozens of examples of states diverting federal funds, often from the nation's largest grant programs, away from targeted purposes. There is no evidence, however, that this information has ever resulted in a significant loss of grant funding for offending jurisdictions. It may be that federal actors are willing to overlook some state discretion in pursuit of the larger policy goal represented by the grant. Equally likely, the political cost of sanctioning state governments is unpalatable for national representatives who may share the preferences of that state or depend on its citizens for reelection.

Notes

CHAPTER ONE: Introduction

1. Glied and Ma (2013).

2. Hiltzik (2014).

3. Governor Dave Heineman. "Medicaid expansion: Just more unaffordable Obamacare." Available at http://www.governor.nebraska.gov/columns/2013/12/06_med_expansion.html.

4. Those states included Arizona, Michigan, Nevada, New Jersey, New Mexico, and Ohio.

5. Calculations by the author using publicly available election returns and the Berry et al. (1998) measure of citizen ideology.

6. See, for example, Nicholson-Crotty (2004).

7. See Zimmerman (1992) or Ingram (1977) for scholarly presentations of these arguments.

8. See Fenno (1976); Mayhew (1974); Smith and Deering (1984) for discussion of the electoral and other motivations.

9. See U.S. GAO (1996) for a discussion of the lengths to which states go to conceal the substitution of federal for own-source funds in the Medicaid program.

10. See, for example, Rich (1989) and Nicholson-Crotty (2004).

11. See Volden (2005, 2007).

12. Nicholson-Crotty (2004).

13. Gramlich (1977): 219.

14. Bickers and Stein (2000); Balla et al. (2002).

15. Bickers and Stein (1996); Larcinese et al. (2006). See Grossman (1994); though see Feld and Schaltegger (2005) for the argument that direct democracy can serve as a constraint on the ability to do so.

16. E. Posner (1996); Bickers and Stein (2000).

17. Zimmerman (2005); Fossett (1983). But see Nathan (1983) for a more nuanced definition of what it means to be dependent on federal aid. He suggests that jurisdictions only become unable to give up grant money when they have gotten in the habit of supplanting general revenue with it.

18. The metaphor was first popularized by the then governor of North Carolina Terry Sanford (D) and later refined and tested by federalism scholars; see, for example, Bowman (1985); Krane (1993). In another (though distinct) bureaucratically

focused argument, Volden (1999) suggests that welfare administrators in the states push for and secure program expansions in response to increases in federal grants but do not push for similar contractions in times of decrease. This, he suggests, minimizes the functional effect of politicized changes in grant aid.

19. See, for example, Bradford and Oates (1971); Chubb (1985b); Gramlich (1977); though see Gamkhar and Ali (2008) for the argument that the enforcement of federal restrictions on grant expenditure does not necessarily correlate with less supplantation.

20. Nathan and Doolittle (1984, 1985). See also Liebschutz, Lurie, and Small (1983).

21. Arnold (1979); Bickers and Stein (1996); Levitt and Snyder (1995); Rich (1989); Rundquist and Carsey (2002).

22. Nicholson-Crotty (2004).

23. Nicholson-Crotty, Theobald, and Wood (2005).

24. Peterson (1981). This specific taxonomy is developed in Peterson (1995) through an extensive survey of the literatures in fiscal federalism and distributive politics. Much of that work has already been reviewed herein, particularly in the section on the motivations of federal politicians for grant distribution.

25. Volden (2005, 2007).

26. See Stein 1990.

27. Nicholson-Crotty and Theobald (2010); Nicholson-Crotty, Staley, and Ritchey (2011).

28. See, for example, Gronke (1999); though see Herron and Theodos (2004) for the argument that electoral motivations may trump party loyalty in state-level decision making.

29. See, for example, Gais and Fosset (2005); Weissert and Weissert (2008); Thompson and Burke (2007).

30. See, for example, Greve (1999).

31. This is the core of Madison's "diversity" hypothesis presented in Federalist No. 10 in the *Federalist Papers*.

32. This is the core of the arguments attributed to George Clinton in *In Opposition to the Destruction of State's Rights* (1787).

33. Bowman and Krause (2003); Walker (2000); Zimmerman (1991, 1992, 2005).

34. Chubb (1985a); Conlan (1986); Grodzins (1966); Haider (1974); Lowi (1978); Malaby and Webber (1991); O'Brien (1993); Posner (1998, 2005).

35. See, for example, Crowley (2000); Soss et al. (2001); Weaver (1996).

36. Weschler (1954): 518. Perhaps the best-known articulation of the political safeguards thesis came in *Garcia v. San Antonio MTA* (1985, 469 U.S. 528), where Justice Harry Blackmun suggested in the majority opinion that there was little need for the Court to establish an inviolate principle of "states' rights" or to intervene in order to protect the sovereignty of the states. He argued that the structure of the federal government and process of selecting national officials within a federalist system were

themselves sufficient to "insulate the interests of the states" from excessive federal intrusion.

37. Devins (2004); Elazar (1998); Prakash and Yoo (2001); Yoo (1996).

38. Prakash (2002).

39. Nicholson-Crotty (2009).

40. Craig and Inman (1982); Derthick (1975b); Gramlich (1977); Ingram (1977b); Oberg (1997); Posner and Wrightson (1996); Wilde (1968). Using models of collective choice, some have predicted that, with certain group preference orderings, formula or lump-sum funds can lead to a greater increase in jurisdictional spending than more restrictive grants (Bradford and Oates 1971; Goetz and McKnew 1972).

41. However, there is a large and related literature on grant asymmetries; for example, see Gamkhar and Oates (1996).

42. See, for example, Bailey and Connolly (1998); GAO 1996; Gramlich (1989); Hines and Thaler (1995). Indeed, some studies suggest that the amount is actually much closer to 0 and that observed flypaper effects are simply statistical artifacts that arise because authors mistakenly treat the award of federal funds as exogenous to state behavior and conditions (Becker 1996; Gordon 2004; Knight 2002; Megdal 1987; Milligan and Smart 2005).

43. Interestingly, when economists look at this variation, the most common question is why so much subnational spending? These studies begin with the assumption that all state politicians have a preference to supplant state spending with federal, allowing them to return as much grant money as possible to citizens in the form of lower taxes. They then ask why, if jurisdictions treat grants as income, they spend so much more in response to that windfall than the 5 to 10% that traditional economic theory would suggest is the marginal propensity of subnational governments to spend out of income. Alternatively, when political scientists look at the variability and grant effectiveness, they often ask why there is so little jurisdictional spending. They tend to take as their starting point the observation that since the demise of revenue sharing, the vast majority of federal grants are supposed to stimulate own-source spending, regardless of the specificity regarding the policy area in which the funds are to be spent.

44. Chubb (1985b).

45. Courant et al. (1979); Logan (1986); Oates (1979); Turnbull (1998).

46. McGuire (1975); Romer and Rosenthal (1980); Volden (1999).

47. Nicholson-Crotty (2004).

48. Nicholson-Crotty and Theobald (2010); Brooks and Smith (2010). The Brooks and Smith result accords with Volden's (2007) proposition that grant impact will be larger in jurisdictions with limited ability to raise revenue. This suggests that the theory may be most accurate in the cases where jurisdictions are deciding how much of a grant to spend (as in the case of block grants), rather than how much to raise own-source spending in response to a grant (as in the case of matching grants).

49. Chubb (1988); Kenney (1983); Levernier (1992); Peltzman (1987).

50. Cohen and King (2004); Niemi, Stanley, and Vogel (1995); Partin (1995).

51. See Atkeson and Partin (1995); Stein (1990); Svoboda (1995).

CHAPTER TWO: A Political Theory of Fiscal Federalism in the States

1. See, for example, Nicholson-Crotty (2004).

2. GAO (1996).

3. GAO (2008).

4. See Rodden (2006) for a nice review.

5. See, for example, Careaga and Weingast (2000); Grossman and West (1994); Oates (1991).

6. Delorme and Andre (1983); Ellwood and Guetzkow (2009); Holsey and Borcherding (1997); D. Mueller (2003).

7. See, for example, Franzese (2002a); Petry et al. (1999).

8. See Alesina (1998) and Imbeau et al. (2001) for reviews.

9. Hibbs (1987a).

10. This is reflected in the responses of members of these classes to survey questions, though the empirical evidence suggests that the impact of high inflation even on these groups is quite modest (Hibbs 1987a). Hibbs (1977) introduces the argument outlined in this paragraph. He provides the most thorough explication in 1987a and extends and reviews key elements of the argument in 1986, 1987b, 1992, and 1994.

11. Hibbs (1987a): 2.

12. Cusack (1999, 2000); Franzese (1999, 2002b); Jonsson (1995); Oatley (1999); Sieg (1997); Simmons (1996); Vaubel (1997).

13. Garrett (1995, 1998); Hallerberg and Basinger (1998); Swank (1992).

14. Borg and Castles (1981); Castles (1981, 1982, 1986, 1989); Castles and McKinlay (1979); Cusack (1997); Franzese (2002a).

15. Boix (2000); Clark (2002); Clark and Hallerberg (2000); Clark, Golder, and Golder (2002); Clark et al. (1998); Hahm (1996); Hahm et al. (1996); Hallerberg et al. (2001); Ross (1997).

16. Alesina, Roubini, and Cohen (1997).

17. Most widely recognized of these is Nordhaus's (1975) "Political Business Cycle," but see also MacRae (1977) and Tufte (1978). These early theories were built around the Phillips curve, which represents the empirical relationship between inflation and unemployment. Classic macro-economic theory proposed a stable relationship between the two, which allows policymakers to "create" higher employment by raising spending and thus inflation or vice-versa.

18. Arcelus and Meltzer (1975); Bloom and Price (1975); Fair (1978, 1982, 1988); and Hibbs (1987a).

19. Ahmad (1983); Beck (1982, 1987); Golden and Poterba (1980); Haynes and Stone (1988, 1989, 1990, 1994); Lachler (1978, 1982); Lewis-Beck (1988); MacRae (1981); McCallum (1978); Thompson and Zuck (1983).

20. Alesina and Rosenthal (1995); Alesina and Sachs (1988); Alesina, Cohen, and Roubini (1992, 1993); Alesina, Roubini, and Cohen (1997); Alt and Chrystal (1983).

21. See Alesina et al. (1993); Ellis and Thomas (1991); Heckelman and Berument (1998); Lohmann (1998, 1999); Rogoff (1990); Rogoff and Sibert (1988); Sieg (1997).

22. Tufte (1978).

23. Alesina (1988); Alesina et al. (1992, 1997); Ames (1987); Beck (1987); Ben-Porath (1975); Block (2001a, b); Block et al. (2001); Brender (1999); Clark (2002); Fouda (1997); Franzese (1999; 2002a, b); Gonzalez (1999a, b; 2000); Harrinvirta and Mattila (2001); Keech and Pak (1989); Khemani (2000); Krueger and Turan (1993); Maloney and Smirlock (1981); Moyo (1999); Price (1998); Schuknecht (1999, 2000); Schultz (1995); Sheffrin (1989); Shi and Svensson (2001); Wright (1974).

24. Unlike the case with partisan cycles, previous scholarship has not uncovered consistent evidence of electoral cycles in macro-economic outcomes such as inflation or employment.

25. Franzese (2002a): 407.

26. Acosta and Coppedge (2001); Alt (1985); Blais et al. (1993, 1996); Franzese (1999; 2002a, b); Tsebelis (2002); Way (2000).

27. Frey and Schneider (1978a, b; 1979).

28. See, for example, Renaud and van Winden (1987).

29. See, for example, Devine (1985); Petry et al. (1999); Schultz (1995); Tellier (2006).

30. Alesina, Roubini, and Cohen (1997).

31. Arcelus and Meltzer (1975); Fair (1988); Hibbs (1987); Stigler (1973).

32. Anderson (2000); Lewis-Beck and Paldam (2000).

33. Lowery, Alt, and Ferree (1998); Neimi, Stanley, and Vogel (1995); though see Chubb (1988); Kenney (1983); Peltzman (1987); and Stein (1990) for the argument that national economic conditions or the popularity of a president of the same party may have a larger impact.

34. Cohen and King (2004); Leyden and Borelli (1995).

35. Canes-Wrone, Brady, Cogan (2002).

36. See, for example, Lees-Marshment (2001); Needham (2005); Petrocik (1996).

37. Numerous state-level actors were interviewed for this project. Their selection and responses are discussed in greater detail at the end of the chapter.

38. Schneider and Jacoby (1996).

39. Gais and Fosset (2005).

40. Thompson and Burke (2007): 971.

41. Thompson and Burke (2008); Weissert and Weissert (2006).

42. Gais and Fossett (2005).

43. Information gathered from Centers for Medicare and Medicaid by the author. See http://www.medicaid.gov/Medicaid-CHIP-Program-Information/By-Topics /Waivers/Waivers.html.

44. Archibald and Feldman (2006); Erikson, Wright, and McIver (1989); Jacoby and Schneider (2001); Stucky and Heimer (2007).

45. Nice (1987).

46. See, for example, Gramlich (1977).

47. Fiorina (1977).

48. See, for example, Campbell (2008); Farah and Klein (1989); Finkel (1993); Holbrook and McClurg (2005).

49. Though see Abramowitz (1995) for the argument that abortion policy played a key role in the 1992 presidential contest.

50. See, for example, Jessee (2010) for work at the individual level.

51. The expected value of representing public opinion in stated policy priorities is a function of the clarity of the public's preferences on an issue, the perceived competence of one party versus another in dealing with that issue, and the risk a party might incur by emphasizing one issue over another, among other factors.

52. Bertelli and John (2013): 170.

53. The authors suggest that the negative impact on vote share under conditions of extreme partisanship may also be due to the public's taste for relative stability in the government's policy portfolio.

54. Jacoby and Schneider (2001)

55. Collins and Gerber (2006). These authors study the "nonentitlement" portion of CDBG.

56. Beyle (1999); Bowling and Ferguson (2001); Clynch and Lauth (1991); Gosling (1994); Hedge (1998); Brudney and Hebert (1987); Hebert, Brudney, and Wright (1983); Rosenthal (1998); Woods (2004); though see Abney and Lauth (1983): 221, for the argument that governors are sometimes "personally incapable or disinclined" to exercise their authority over agencies.

57. Dometrius (2002); Sigelman and Dometrius (1988).

58. See, for example, Sharkansky (1968).

59. See, for example, Abney and Lauth (1987); Dometrius and Wright (2010).

60. Hoffman (2006).

61. Gosling (2003); Thurmaier and Willoughby (2001).

62. Kousser and Phillips (2012).

63. This assertion is based on interviews by the author with state officials. More details from these interviews are presented in the next section of this chapter.

64. See Barrilleaux and Berkman (2003); Beyle (1986); and Clynch and Lauth (1991) for detailed discussions of these powers and their implications for gubernatorial influence.

65. See Beyle (1986); Digler, Krause, and Moffet (1995); and Dometrius (1979) for further discussion of the determination and the import of the appointment power.

66. Beyle (2004); Krause, Lewis, and Douglas (2006).

67. As an example, Jacoby and Schneider (2001) demonstrate that Medicaid administrators within the states have significant influence over benefits and services offered but acknowledge that bureaucrats must ultimately answer to the legislature for their choices.

68. See, for example, Gerber, Maestes, and Dometrius (2005); Woods (2006).

69. See, for example, Bernick and Wiggins (1991); Beyle (1990, 1992, 1996); Brudney and Hebert (1987); Dilger, Krause, and Moffett (1995); Edwards and Wayne (1990); Fett (1994); Fiorina (1984); Gross (1991); Jacobson (1987); Kingdon (1984); Mueller (1985); Neustadt (1980); Schlesinger (1965); Sigelman and Dometrius (1988). It is important to note that while many of the studies cited here were actually concerned with presidential success in Congress, the insights from them have been routinely applied to studies of governors in the American states.

70. Beyle (1996, 1992); Bond and Fleisher (1990); Bowling and Ferguson (2001); Crew (1992); Gleiber and Shull (1992); Kingdon (1984); Morehouse (1996).

71. Ferguson (2003).

72. For the latter characteristic I divided the states into quartiles based on the proportion of total revenue made up by federal grants. Ultimately, the sample of states consisted of one from each quartile of "dependence"; one from each of four regions (West, Midwest, South, and Northeast); two headed by Republicans and two by Democrats; two with Unified government; and two where at least one chamber in the legislature is controlled by a different party than the governor's.

73. Interviews were conducted between June and October 2012. The discussion here mentions the position (e.g., Deputy Director of the Department of Education, State Representative, etc.) of the interviewee and the region of their state (West, South, etc.) but does not identify the state by name. Doing so would make it easy to identify the individual and violate the expectation of confidentiality. As an additional protection for subjects, titles have been changed in cases where they or the name of the agency with which an individual is affiliated are unique enough to allow ascription.

CHAPTER THREE: The Strategic Pursuit of Federal Grants

1. Girard (2004).

2. Boonstra (2003); Society for Adolescent Medicine (2006); Trenholm et al. (2007).

3. Stein (2010).

4. P. J. Huffstutter, "States refraining from abstinence-only sex education: Refuse to accept dictates made by White House." *Los Angeles Times*, April 9, 2007. http://www.boston.com/news/nation/articles/2007/04/09/states_refraining_from_absti nence_only_sex_education. Accessed October 25, 2011.

5. "States turn down abstinence education grants." *USA Today*, June 24, 2008. http://www.usatoday.com/news/education/2008-06-24-abstinence-grants_N.htm. Accessed April 15, 2012.

6. Balla et al. (2002); Bickers and Stein (1996, 2000); Dixit and Londregan (1998); Larcinese et al. (2006) Lindbeck and Weibull (1993).

7. Arnold (1979); Bickers and Stein (1996); Levitt and Snyder (1995); Rich (1989); Rundquist and Carsey (2002); Volden (2007).

8. Bleakley et al. (2006).

9. Ten policies were originally sampled, but two were dropped because state governments were not the primary applicants for the funding, and one was dropped because the bulk of the funding was actually awarded by formula.

10. See Thompson and Burke (2008).

11. In FY2008 they represented 73%, while in FY2009 they represented 84% (GAO 2009).

12. There were also dozens of region or place specific grants during this period, such as the Lower Colorado River Multi-Species Conservation Program and the Potomac Highlands Implementation Program. Additionally, there were also hundreds of grants targeted at recipients other than state governments. However, I restrict the discussion here to programs for which states were the primary applicants and all states might have received funding.

13. See Nicholson-Crotty (2012).

14. Perry, Rick. 2010. "Perry: Rejecting Race to the Top Funds Was an Easy Call," *Statesman.com*. Available at http://www.statesman.com/opinion/perry-rejecting -race-to-the-top-funds-was-214066.html. Accessed October 25, 2011.

15. John O'Connor, "Everything You Need to Know about Education and the Florida 2012 GOP Primary," *State Impact: A Reporting Project of Local Public Media and NPR* (Jan. 23, 2012). Available at http://stateimpact.npr.org/florida/2012/01/23/ everything-you-need-to-know-about-education-and-the-florida-2012-gop-primary/. Accessed May 6, 2012. It is interesting to note, however, that Gingrich actually had relatively nice things to say about RTTT before he declared that he would seek the nomination. See Mary Kate Carey, "Republicans and Democrats Can Embrace Obama's Race to the Top for Education: With an unacceptable status quo, education reform is winning over both sides," *US News and World Report* (Dec. 2, 2009). Available at http://www.usnews.com/opinion/articles/2009/12/02/republicans-and -democrats-can-embrace-obamas-race-to-the-top-for-education.

16. Feldman (2010).

17. Metz (2010).

18. Brill (2010).

19. See Nicholson-Crotty and Staley (2012). For states that did not have a State of the State Address in 2008, we analyzed the 2007 speech.

20. In order to check the reliability of the data, six states were randomly selected and double coded. This exceeds the 10% standard established by Riffe, Lacy, and Fico (2005). Education claims achieved reliability with an alpha of .90.

21. Available at www.followthemoney.org.

22. Assigned grades were a function of the degree to which policies facilitated or restricted the establishment of charters as well as the accountability measures that were put in place for these organizations. In one departure from the CER measure, we code states with no charter-specific laws as an F because there is no state mechanism to help create these organizations and the lack of statute often complicates state oversight. Available at www.edreform.com/_upload/cer_state_scorecard.pdf.

23. It should be noted that the impact of NAEP math performance is also larger

than gubernatorial partisanship if math and reading scores are entered into the model separately rather than as a combined score as they are here.

24. See, for example, Gais and Fosset (2005).

25. Fording (2003).

26. Thompson and Burke (2007); Weissert and Weissert (2008).

27. Thompson and Burke (2008).

28. See Hansen and Heaney (1997).

29. See Heclo (2001).

30. Fording (2003).

31. Previous models have used dichotomous variables to capture this interaction (Republican No Election, Republican Election, Democrat Election), which allows for a somewhat more precise observation of the behavior of members of both parties. However, the year fixed effects included in this model introduce significant collinearity with one of these indicators, causing it to be dropped from the analysis. As a result, I model the interaction by including the main effects and one multiplicative interaction term.

32. This is an RTS-based measure created by the ACIR and extended by Tannenwald (1999).

33. See W. D. Berry et al. (1998).

34. Available at www.unc.edu/~beyle/gubnewpwr.html.

35. The results do not change if I estimate a linear time trend instead. The limited time frame precludes the inclusion of state fixed effects. Similarly, the limited time frame and the inclusion of year fixed effects requires that some control variables, including presidential election year, governor is same party as the President, and partisan control of the legislature, be dropped from the analysis due to lack of variation or collinearity.

36. Arizona and Vermont operate their Medicaid long-term care program under a Section 1115 waiver and are not, therefore, included in this analysis. See Kaiser Commission on Medicaid and the Uninsured (2011).

37. Houser et al. (2006).

38. This is consistent with the finding in the literature that Republicans enroll as many persons in 1915(c) programs as do Democrats but that the expenditure per participant is considerably lower in Republican-led states (see Thompson and Burke 2008).

CHAPTER FOUR: The Strategic Expenditure of Federal Grants

1. Press Release of Nov. 30, 2011. http://bennelson.senate.gov/press/press_releases/nelson-says-state-should-either-return-money-or-create-health-insurance-exchanges.cfm. Accessed May 29, 2014.

2. GAO (1996).

3. GAO (2004).

4. See, for example, Bradford and Oates (1968); Gramlich (1977).

5. GAO (2004).

6. See, for example, GAO (1995; 2010; 2011); Nicholson-Crotty and Theobald (2011). However, see Volden (2007) for the argument that states that can spend more of their own money on a public good may also spend more federal money in the targeted area.

7. See Nicholson-Crotty (2004); Nicholson-Crotty, Theobald, and Wood (2006); Nicholson-Crotty (2009).

8. Of course, any observed grant expenditure relationships will be conditional on institutional factors such as divided government, executive fragmentation, and gubernatorial power that constrain or facilitate the ability of governors to translate grants into political resources.

9. Alt and Lowry (1994; 2000); Dye (1966); Ringquist and Garand (1999).

10. F. Berry and W. Berry (1992); Camobreco (1998); Kiewiet and McCubbins (1985); McAtee, Yackee, and Lowery (2003).

11. See, for example, Bradford and Oates (1971); Case, Hines, and Rosen (1993); Gramlich and Galper (1973).

12. Nicholson-Crotty (2009).

13. See, for example, Tannenwald (1999).

14. See Advisory Commission on Intergovernmental Relations (1982) for an early and cogent explanation of the RTS approach.

15. See, for example, Ambrosius (1989); W. Berry and Fording (1987); Due and Mikesell (1994); Wohlenberg (1992). These include that the measure is not well suited to comparisons over time, that the choice of taxable categories is arbitrary, and the assumption that different tax bases can be exploited independently.

16. See Compsen (2003); Mikesell (2007).

17. Berry and Fording (1997); Tannenwald (1999); The ACIR, which created the longest RTS series, did so up to 1991 but typically did not collect the measure every year. Fortunately, scholars have estimated values in the missing years, creating a continuous series between 1960 and 1991 and, using the same methodology as the ACIR, extended the series to include 1994 and 1996. I estimate the missing values for 1992, 1993, and 1995 using linear interpolation, which Berry and Fording suggest is a reliable method for the estimation of tax effort after 1975.

18. The first differences estimator also has the advantage of eliminating bias from time-constant unobserved heterogeneity and of isolating the effect of within, rather than between, state variation.

19. The first difference and fixed effects models are identical if T = 2, but they diverge with a greater number of time periods.

20. See Mikesell (2007) for an elaboration.

21. See, for example, Besley and Case (1995). The series is not integrated and thus does not need to be differenced. The analysis contains both year and state fixed effects.

22. F. Berry and W. Berry (1992).

23. Barro (1986).

24. Stonecash (1981, 1983).

25. The coefficient is jointly significant with the other components of the interaction.

26. These results are robust to the use of the lagged difference for grants.

27. Nicholson-Crotty (2004).

28. Pew (2014).

29. For a complete catalogue of programs, see http://www.fhwa.dot.gov.

30. See Jacoby and Schneider (2001).

31. The figure excludes amounts allocated for collection expenses, nonhighway purposes, and mass transit.

32. There are some exceptions, of course, such as the Juvenile Mentorship program and the Residential Substance Abuse Treatment for State Prisoners program, which might be more attractive to liberal than to conservative constituencies. However, the majority of DOJ grants, particularly the larger ones, are clearly focused on producing relatively conservative justice outcomes (higher arrests, more convictions, longer sentences, etc.).

33. For example, if we pick two of the largest DOJ grants, Byrne Formula grants have matching requirements, while Crime Victims Assistance funds do not.

34. Mayhew (1974). This refers only to *willing* disclosures, of course. Politicians might be forced by opponents or circumstances to reveal things that are politically detrimental, but there is no rational incentive to willingly claim credit for an accomplishment unless there is some payoff assumed.

35. Coffey (2005): 88. See also Beyle (1988); Morehouse (1996).

36. All differences reported here are significant at the .1 level or below.

37. These results also suggest that governors from both parties advertise spending on distributive policies more than that on redistribution, which matches well with expectations regarding state incentives developed by Peterson (1995).

38. This quote and all others discussed in this section are drawn from the State of the State Address for the state and year identified in the text. The full texts of these speeches were available online at Stateline.org when this project was being written and were last accessed January 2011. They are no longer online but are available by request from Stateline, which is now a subsidiary of the Pew Charitable Trust.

39. Despite criticism for overseeing the largest tax increase in the state's history, he was widely praised for the success of his Third Frontier initiative in attracting new businesses and creating jobs. See "Ohio Third Frontier creates $6.6 billion in economic impact, 41,300 jobs," Med City News, retrieved Feb. 10, 2012; and "Ohio Remains Nation's No. 1 Choice for Business Development," Reuters, retrieved Feb. 10, 2012.

40. "The Columbus Dispatch—Local/State," Ohioelects.com. 2010-11-30. http://www.ohioelects.com/poll/?story=dispatch/2006/09/24/20060924-A10-01.html. Retrieved Feb. 10, 2012. Julie Carr Smyth (2006-09-13), "GOP loyalists back Democrat in governor race," Associated Press. http://www.cantonrep.com/index.php?ID=307576&Category=13. Retrieved Feb. 10, 2012.

41. Ted Strickland, "Reforming Education for Ohio's Future." https://www.csu ohio.edu/offices/assessment/ReformingOhioEducationSystemforthe21stCentury.pdf. Retrieved Feb. 11, 2012. Marilyn Karfeld, "Governor's race too close to call," *Cleveland Jewish News*, Nov. 3, 2010.

42. "Owens tenure coming to an end." *Denver Post.* Dec. 12, 2006. http://www .denverpost.com/ci_4813328. Retrieved Feb. 12, 2012.

43. Morehouse (1981; 1998).

44. A small literature has investigated the allocation of Small Cities Community Development Block Grant funding since the Reagan administration shifted control of that program to the states. This literature has found that both the ways state agencies structured those competitions and local grants capacity had a significant influence on the awards process (Collins and Gerber 2006). It has also found that the types of communities receiving awards changed after the devolution and that states shifted funding toward public works and other projects that were more distributive in nature and away from the classic focus on housing rehabilitation and other redistributive goals (Fossett 1987; Krane 1987). These studies do not, however, test whether state agencies distribute CBDG funds in a way that would allow governors to reward fellow partisans, particularly in the legislature.

45. C. Berry, Burden, and Howell (2010).

46. Aldrich (1995); Cox and McCubbins (2007); Galvin (2009); Jacobson, Kernell, and Lazarus (2004).

47. C. Berry, Burden, and Howell (2010); Larcinese et al. (2006).

48. As noted in chapter 2, interview subjects consistently reported that legislatures often took an interest in long-ignored programs after they were bundled into controversial pieces of legislation such as the Affordable Care Act.

49. Larcinese et al. (2006): 447.

50. See, for example, C. Berry, Burden, and Howell (2010); Bickers and Stein (1996, 2000).

51. They do so because they are interested in the impact of shared partisanship between governors and presidents as well as between the chief executive and members of Congress.

52. Carsey et al. (2007).

53. Ideally, the analysis would also control for the percentage of legislators from the majority party in the state legislature, but this is perfectly collinear with the measure of shared party with the governor.

CHAPTER FIVE: Grants and the Electoral Connection

1. The allocation was increased to $831 billion in 2010.

2. A total of $335 billion had been obligated to approved projects by January 2011, and an additional $93 billion had been "spent" by that time in the form of tax cuts. http://online.wsj.com/search/term.html?KEYWORDS=LOUISE+RADNOFSKY&by linesearch=trueRadnofsky (2010).

3. Atkeson and Partin (1995); Carsey and Wright (1998); Chubb (1988); Cohen and King (2004); Cummins (2009); Peltzman (1987).

4. Cummins (2009).

5. Abramowitz (1995); Brians and Greene (2004); Cook, Jelen, and Wilcox (1994); Cummins (2009); Gimpel (1998); MacDonald, Rabinowitz, and Listhaug (1995).

6. Kenney (1983).

7. Ibid.

8. See Chubb (1988); Stein (1990).

9. Atkeson and Partin (1995).

10. Niemi, Stanley, and Vogel (1995).

11. Tompkins (1988).

12. See Atkeson and Partin (1995); Morehouse (1998); Niemi, Stanley, and Vogel (1995).

13. The expected value of representing public opinion in stated policy priorities is a function of the clarity of the public's preferences on an issue, the perceived competence of one party versus another in dealing with that issue, and the risk a party might incur by emphasizing one issue over another, among other factors.

14. Bertelli and John (2013): 170.

15. See, for example, Cummins (2009); Partin (2002).

16. See Stults and Winters (2005) for a particularly thorough review of this literature.

17. See, for example, Partin (2002).

18. Results discussed below hold in the presence of a time trend, which does not reach statistical significance.

19. See Kenney and Rice (1983); King (2001); Svoboda (1995).

20. Crew et al. (2002); Hansen (1999); Howell and Vanderleeuw (1990); Orth (2001).

21. Adams and Squire (2001); Crew and Weiher (1996); MacDonald and Sigelman (1999).

22. Cohen and King (2004).

23. Ibid.

24. Beyle, Niemi, and Sigelman (2002); Crew and Weiher (1996); Hansen (1999).

25. Collected by Beyle, Niemi, and Sigelman (2002).

26. This requires some compromises relative to previous work because the values for individual states and years reflect different numbers of polls from different pollsters. As a result, it is more difficult to take account of variations in question wording and response categories. However, it also has advantages over previous work because the variable more closely matches independent and control variables and because the use of the state year as the unit of analysis allows for the analysis to control for the temporal dependence in approval.

27. Beyle (1968). The measure ranges from 1 to 5 and captures the governor's power over budget proposals and appointments, the extent of veto power, and so forth.

28. Grants become insignificant at slightly less than 1-sd greater than the mean level of partisan homogeneity, which means that it is significant in roughly that proportion of states if we assume a normal distribution.

29. King (1983): 247.

30. Kousser and Phillips (2012): 5.

31. See, for example, Dye (1969); Morehouse (1981); Rosenthal (1990).

32. See, for example, Alt and Lowery (1994); Schneider (1989).

33. See, for example, Ferguson (2003); Morehouse (1996).

34. Kousser and Phillips (2012): 4.

35. Two other studies have created success indices for at least a majority of states. The measure offered by Ferguson (2003) is the most comprehensive covering all 50 states. The measure of legislative success created by Fording, Woods, and Prince (2002) is the second most comprehensive of comparable measures, covering 37 states. Fording et al. were kind enough to share their measure of success, and an analysis suggests that grants correlate positively with success in those states where governors had relatively small agendas. The effect becomes insignificant, however, when the governor's agenda reaches approximately 1-sd larger than the mean size. Model available from the author upon request.

36. The authors also create the measure for 2006, but data falls outside the scope of the data for this project, which runs through 2005.

37. Kousser and Phillips (2012): 111.

38. I also estimate models that use the annual change in grants per capita as the independent variable in order to confirm the robustness of the results and reduce the potential spuriousness arising from factors that influence both grants and success, but that cannot be controlled for in a model with such limited degrees of freedom. The findings are essentially unchanged except that the differenced measure falls below traditional levels of statistical significance in the model of success on budget bills.

39. Squire (2007).

40. See Ferguson (2003).

41. These are created using Clarify (see Tomz, Wittenberg, and King 2003), which generates 1,000 simulations for each parameter and then simulates predicted values of legislative success across the range of the grant measure. The predicted values account for both predictive and estimation uncertainty.

CHAPTER SIX: Conclusion

1. Zimmerman (1996).

2. Bob Riley (R-AL), Bobby Jindal (R-LA), Tim Pawlenty (R-MN), Haley Barbour (R-MS), Mark Sanford (R-SC), Rick Perry (R-TX), and Sarah Palin (R-AK).

3. See, for example, Kaiser Health News (2011); Sack (2011).

4. However, it is important to note that only three of five such relationships were statistically significant.

5. Data compiled by Eric Ostermeier at the Humphrey School of Public Affairs, University of Minnesota. See http://blog.lib.umn.edu/cspg/smartpolitics/2010/08/which_states_host_the_most_com.php for the full report.

6. 5% is the marginal effect, given a 2-standard deviation change in grants.

7. Buchannan and Tollock (1962).

References

Abney, Glenn, and Thomas Lauth. 1987. "Perceptions of the Impact of Governors and Legislatures in the Appropriations Process." *Western Political Quarterly* 40:335–342.

Abramowitz, Alan. 1995. "It's Abortion Stupid: Policy Voting in the 1992 Presidential Election." *Journal of Politics* 57:176–186.

Acosta, A. M., and M. Coppedge. 2001. "Political Determinants of Fiscal Discipline in Latin America, 1979–1998." Paper presented at Annual Meeting of the Latin American Studies Associations, Washington, DC, Sept. 5–8.

Adams, Greg D., and Peverill Squire. 2001. "A Note on the Dynamics and Idiosyncrasies of Gubernatorial Popularity." *State Politics and Policy Quarterly* 1 (4): 380–393.

Advisory Commission on Intergovernmental Relations. 1982. *Tax Capacity of the Fifty States: Methodology and Estimates.* Washington, DC: U.S. Government Printing Office.

Ahmad, K. V. 1983. "An Empirical Study of Politico-Economic Interaction in the United States." *Review of Economics and Statistics* 65:170–177.

Aldrich, John. 1995. *Why Parties? The Origin and Transformation of Parties in America.* Chicago: University of Chicago Press.

Alesina, A. 1988. "Macroeconomics and Politics." *National Bureau of Economic Research Macroeconomic Annual* 3:13–61.

———. 1998. "Governability and Economic Performance." In *Justice Delayed: Judicial Reform in Latin America,* ed. Edmundo Jarquín and Fernando Carrillo, chap. 8. Washington, DC: Inter-American Development Bank.

Alesina, A., G. Cohen, and N. Roubini. 1992. "Macroeconomic Policies and Elections in OECD Democracies." *Economics and Politics* 4:1–30.

———. 1993. "Electoral Business Cycles in Industrial Democracies." *European Journal of Political Economy* 23:1–25.

Alesina, A., J. Londregan, and H. Rosenthal. 1993. "A Model of the Political Economy of the United States." *American Political Science Review* 87:12–33.

Alesina, A., and H. Rosenthal. 1995. *Partisan Politics, Divided Government, and the Economy.* Cambridge, UK: Cambridge University Press.

Alesina, A., N. Roubini, and G. Cohen. 1997. *Political Cycles and the Macroeconomy.* Cambridge, MA: MIT Press.

Alesina, A., and J. Sachs. 1988. "Political Parties and Business Cycle in the United States." *Journal of Money Credit and Banking* 20:63–82.

Alt, James E. 1985. "Political Parties, World Demand, and Unemployment: Domestic and International Sources of Economic Activity." *American Political Science Review* 79:1016–1040.

Alt, James, and K. A. Chrystal. 1983. *Political Economics.* Berkeley: University of California Press.

Alt, James, and Robert Lowry. 1994. "Divided Government, Fiscal Institutions, and Budget Deficits: Evidence from the States." *American Political Science Review* 88:811–828.

———. 2000. "A Dynamic Model of State Budget Outcomes under Partisan Divided Government." *Journal of Politics* 62:1035–1069.

Ambrosius, Margery. 1989. "The Role of Occupational Interests in State Economic Development Policy." *Western Political Quarterly* 41:53–68.

Ames, B. 1987. *Political Survival.* Berkeley: University of California Press.

Anderson, Christopher J. 2000. "Economic Voting and Political Context: A Comparative Perspective." *Electoral Studies* 19 (2): 151–170.

Arcelus, F., and A. Meltzer. 1975. "The Effect of Aggregate Economic Variables on Congressional Elections." *American Political Science Review* 69:1232–1239.

Archibald, R., and D. Feldman. 2006. "State Higher Education and the Tax Revolt." *Journal of Higher Education* 77:618–644.

Arnold, R. Douglas. 1979. *Congress and the Bureaucracy: A Theory of Influence.* New Haven, CT: Yale University Press.

Atkeson, Lonna Rae, and Randall W. Partin. 1995. "Economic and Referendum Voting: A Comparison of Gubernatorial and Senatorial Elections." *American Political Science Review* 89:99–107.

Bailey, Stephen, and Stephen Connolly. 1997. "The Flypaper Effect: Identifying Research for Further Areas." *Public Choice* 95:335–361.

Balla, J. Steven, D. Eric Lawrence, Forrest Maltzman, and Lee Sigelman. 2002. "Partisanship, Blame Avoidance, and the Distribution of Legislative Pork." *American Journal of Political Science* 46:515–525.

Barrilleaux, Charles, and Michael Berkman. 2003. "Do Governors Matter? Budgeting Rules and the Politics of State Policymaking." *Political Research Quarterly* 56:409–417.

Barro, R. J. 1986. "Reputation in a Model of Monetary Policy with Incomplete Information." *Journal of Monetary Economics* 17:3–20.

Beck, N. 1982. "Does There Exist a Political Business Cycle? A Box-Tiao Analysis." *Public Choice* 38:205–212.

———. 1987. "Elections and the Fed: Is There a Political Monetary Cycle?" *American Journal of Political Science* 31:194–216.

Becker, Elizabeth. 1996. "The Illusion of Fiscal Illusion: Unsticking the Flypaper Effect." *Public Choice* 86:85–102.

Ben-Porath, Y. 1975. "The Years of Plenty and the Years of Famine—a Political Business." *Kyklos* 28:400–403.

Bernick, E. Lee, and Charles W. Wiggins. 1981. "Executive-Legislative Power Relationships: Perspectives of State Lawmakers." *American Politics Quarterly* 9:467–477.

Berry, Christopher R., Barry C. Burden, and William G. Howell. 2010. "The President and the Distribution of Federal Spending." *American Political Science Review* 104:783–799.

Berry, Frances, and William Berry. 1992. "Tax Innovation in the States: Capitalizing on Political Opportunity." *American Journal of Political Science* 36:715–742.

Berry, Jeffrey. 1977. *Lobbying for People: The Political Behavior of Public Interest Groups.* Princeton, NJ: Princeton University Press.

Berry, William, and Richard Fording. 1997. "Measuring State Tax Capacity and Effort. *Social Science Quarterly* 78:158–166.

Berry, William D., Evan J. Ringquist, Richard C. Fording, and Russell L. Hanson. 1998. "Measuring Citizen and Government Ideology in the American States, 1960–93." *American Journal of Political Science* 42 (1): 327–348.

Bertelli, Anthony, and Peter John. 2013. *Public Policy Investment: Policy Prioritization and British Statecraft.* New York: Oxford University Press.

Besley, Timothy J., and Case, Anne C. 1995. "Incumbent Behavior: Vote Seeking, Tax Setting, and Yardstick Competition," *American Economic Review* 85:25–45.

Beyle, Thad L. 1968. "The Governor's Formal Powers: A View from the Governor's Chair." *Public Administration Review* 28:540–545.

———. 1986. *Re-electing the Governor: The 1982 Elections.* Lanham, MD: University Press of America.

———. 1988. "The Governor as Innovator in the Federal System." *Publius* 18 (3): 131–152.

———. 1990. "Governors." In *Politics in the American States*, ed. Virginia Gray, Harold Jacobs, and Kenneth Vines. 5th ed. Boston: Little, Brown.

———. 1992. *Governors and Hard Times.* Washington, DC: Congressional Quarterly Inc.

———. 1996. *State Government: CQ's Guide to Current Issues and Activities, 1996–97.* Washington, DC: Congressional Quarterly Inc.

———. 1999. "The Governors." In *Politics in the American States: A Comparative Analysis*, ed. Virginia Gray, Russell Hansen, and Herbert Jacob, 194–231. Washington, DC: CQ Press.

Beyle, Thad, Richard G. Niemi, and Lee Sigelman. 2002. "Gubernatorial, Senatorial, and State-Level Presidential Job Approval: The US Official Job Approval Ratings (JAR) Collection." *State Politics and Policy Quarterly* 2 (3): 215–229.

Bickers, Kenneth N., and Robert M. Stein. 1996. "The Electoral Dynamics of the Federal Pork Barrel." *American Journal of Political Science* 40 (4): 1300–1326.

———. 2000. "The Congressional Pork Barrel in a Republican Era." *Journal of Politics* 62 (4): 1070–1086.

Blais, A., D. Blake, and S. Dion. 1993. "Do Parties Make a Difference? Parties and the Size of Government in Liberal Democracies." *American Journal of Political Science* 37:40–62.

———. 1996. "Do Parties Make a Difference? A Reappraisal." *American Journal of Political Science* 40:514–520.

Bleakley, Amy, Michael Hennessy, and Martin Fishbein. 2006. "Public Opinion on Sex Education in US Schools." *Arch Pediatric and Adolescent Medicine* 160:1151–1166.

Block, S. 2001a. "Does Africa Grow Differently?" *Journal of Development Economics* 65:443–467.

———. 2001b. "Elections, Electoral Competitiveness, and Political Budget Cycles in Developing Countries." Working paper. Fletcher School of Law and Diplomacy, Tufts University.

Block, S., K. Ferree, and S. Singh. 2001. "Institutions, Electoral Competitiveness, and Political Business Cycles in Nascent Democracies." Working paper. Fletcher School of Law and Diplomacy, Tufts University.

Bloom, H., and H. Price. 1975. "Voter Response to Short-run Economic Conditions: The Asymmetric Effect of Prosperity and Recession." *American Journal of Political Science* 69:1240–1254.

Boix, C. 2000. "Partisan Governments, the International Economy, and Macroeconomic Policies in OECD countries, 1964–93." *World Politics.* 53:38–73.

Bond, Jon, and Richard Fleisher. 1990. *The President in the Legislative Arena.* Chicago: University of Chicago Press.

Boonstra, H. 2003. "Public Health Advocates Say Campaign to Disparage Condoms Threatens STD Prevention Efforts." *Guttmacher Report on Public Policy,* 6 (1). http://www.guttmacher.org/pubs/tgr/06/1/gr060101.html. Accessed May 31, 2006.

Borg, S. G., and F. G. Castles. 1981. "The Influence of the Political Right on Public Income Maintenance Expenditure and Equality." *Political Studies* 29:604–621.

Bowling, Cynthia, and Margaret Ferguson. 2001. "Divided Government, Interest Representation, and Policy Differences: Competing Explanations of Gridlock in the Fifty States." *Journal of Politics* 63:182–206.

Bowman, Ann. 1985. "Hazardous Waste Management: An Emerging Policy Area within an Emerging Federalism." *Publius* 15:131–144.

Bowman, Ann, and George Krause. 2003. "Power Shift: Measuring Policy Centralization in U.S. intergovernmental relations, 1947–1998." *American Politics Research* 31:301–325.

Bradford, D. F., and W. E. Oates. 1971. "Towards a Predictive Theory of Intergovernmental Grants." *American Economic Review* 61:440–448.

Brender, A. 1999. "The Effect of Fiscal Performance on Local Government Election Results in Israel: 1989–98." Bank Israel Research Department, Discussion Paper, 99.04.

Brians, Craig Leonard, and Steven Greene. 2004. "Elections: Voter Support and Partisans'(Mis)Perceptions of Presidential Candidates' Abortion Views in 2000." *Presidential Studies Quarterly* 34 (2): 412–419.

Brill, Steven. "The Teachers' Unions' Last Stand." 2010. *New York Times Magazine,*

May 17. http://www.nytimes.com/2010/05/23/magazine/23Race-t.html?_r=1&page wanted=all.

Brooks, L., and J. Phillips. 2010. "An Institutional Explanation for the Stickiness of Federal Grants." *Journal of Law, Economics, and Organization* 26:243–264.

Brudney, Jeffrey, and Ted Hebert. 1987. "Controlling Administrative Agencies in a Changing Federal System: Avenues of Gubernatorial Influence." *American Review of Public Administration* 18:135.

Buchanan, James M., and Gordon Tullock. 1962. *The Calculus of Consent.* Ann Arbor: University of Michigan Press.

Camobreco, John. 1998. "Preferences, Fiscal Policies, and the Initiative Process." *Journal of Politics* 60:819–829.

Campbell, James E. 2008. *The American Campaign: U.S. Presidential Campaigns and the National Vote.* 2nd ed. College Station: Texas A&M Press.

Canes-Wrone, Brandice, David Brady, and John Cogan. 2002. "Out of Step, Out of Office: Electoral Accountability and House Member's Voting." *American Political Science Review* 96:127–140.

Careaga, Maite, and Barry Weingast. 2003. "Fiscal Federalism, Good Governance, and Economic Growth in Mexico." In *In Search of Prosperity: Analytical Narratives on Economic Growth,* 399–435. Princeton, NJ: Princeton University Press.

Carsey, Thomas M., William D. Berry, Richard G. Niemi, Lynda W. Powell, and James M. Snyder. 2007. *State Legislative Election Returns, 1967–2003.* ICPSR21480-v1. Chapel Hill: University of North Carolina. doi:10.3886/ICPSR21480.v1.

Case, Anne C., James R. Hines Jr., and Harvey S. Rosen. 1993. "Budget Spillovers and Fiscal Policy Interdependence: Evidence from the States," *Journal of Public Economics* 52:285–307.

Castles, F. G. 1981. "How Does Politics Matter? Structure or Agency in the Determination of Public Policy Outcomes." *European Journal of Political Research* 9:119–132.

———. 1982. "The Impact of Parties on Public Expenditure." In *The Impact of Parties,* ed. F. G. Castles, 21–93. Beverly Hills, CA: Sage.

———. 1986. "Social Expenditure and the Political Right: A Methodological Note." *Eur. J. Polit. Res.* 14:669–676.

———. 1989. "Explaining Public Education Expenditure in OECD Nations." *Eur. J. Polit. Res.* 17:431–448.

Castles F. G., and R. D. McKinlay. 1979. "Public Welfare Provision, Scandinavia and the Sheer Futility of the Sociological Approach to Politics." *British Journal of Political Science* 9:157–171.

Chubb, John. 1985a. "Federalism and the Bias for Centralization." In *The New Direction in American Politics,* ed. John Chubb and Paul Peterson. Washington, DC: Brookings Institution.

———. 1985b. "The Political Economy of Federalism." *American Political Science Review* 79:994–1015.

————. 1988. "Institutions, the Economy, and the Dynamics of State Elections." *American Political Science Review* 82:133–154.

Clark, W. R. 2002. *Capitalism Not Globalism: Capital Mobility, Central Bank Independence, and Political Control of the Economy.* Ann Arbor: University of Michigan Press.

Clark, W. R., M. Golder, and S. Golder. 2002. "Fiscal Policy and the Democratic Process in the European Union." Working paper. Department of Political Science, New York University. http://homepages.nyu.edu/»mrg217/JEUP3.pdf.

Clark, W. R., and M. Hallerberg. 2000. "Mobile Capital, Domestic Institutions, and Electorally Induced Monetary and Fiscal Policy." *American Political Science Review* 94:323–346.

Clynch, Thomas, and Edward Lauth. 1991. *Governors, Legislatures and Budgets: Diversity across the American States.* Westport, CT: Greenwood Press.

Coffey, D. 2005. "Measuring Gubernatorial Ideology: A Content Analysis of State of the State Speeches." *State Politics and Policy Quarterly* 5:88–103.

Cohen, Jeffrey E., and James D. King. 2004. "Relative Unemployment and Gubernatorial Popularity." *Journal of Politics* 66:1267–1282.

Collins, B. K., and B. J. Gerber. 2006. "Moving Beyond the Passive to Active Representative Bureaucracy Transformation: Defining and Assessing the Concept of Delegated Representation." Paper presented at the State Politics Conference. http://0-www.olemiss.edu.umiss.lib.olemiss.edu/depts/political_science/state_politics/conferences/2006/Papers/Collins-Gerber-Moving%20Beyond%20SPP2006.pdf.

Compson, Michael L. 2003. "Historical Estimates of Total Taxable Resources for U.S. States, 1981–2000." *Publius* 33:55–72.

Conlan, T. J. 1986. "Federalism and Competing Values in the Reagan Administration." *Publius* 16:29–48.

Cook, Elizabeth Adell, Ted G. Jelen, and Clyde Wilcox. 1994. "Issue Voting in Gubernatorial Elections: Abortion and Post-Webster Politics." *Journal of Politics* 56:187–199.

Courant, Paul N., Edward M. Gramlich, and Daniel L. Rubinfeld. 1979. "Public Employee Market Power and the Level of Government Spending." *American Economic Review* 69:806–817.

Cox, Gary, and Mathew McCubbins. 1991. "On the Decline of Party Voting in Congress." *Legislative Studies Quarterly* 16:547–570.

————. 2005. *Setting the Agenda: Responsible Party Government in the U.S. House of Representatives.* New York: Cambridge University Press.

————. 2007. *Legislative Leviathan: Party Government in the House.* New York: Cambridge University Press.

Craig, S. G., and R. P. Inman. 1982. "Federal Aid and Public Education: An Empirical Look at the New Fiscal Federalism." *Review of Economics and Statistics* 64:541–552.

Crew, Robert E. 1992. "Understanding Gubernatorial Behavior: A Framework for Analysis." In *Governors and Hard Times,* ed. Thad Beyle. Washington, DC: Congressional Quarterly.

Crew, Robert E., Jr., David Branham, Gregory R. Weiher, and Ethan Berick. 2002. "Political Events in a Model of Gubernatorial Approval." *State Politics and Policy Quarterly* 2 (Fall): 283–297.

Crew, Robert E., Jr., and Gregory R. Weiher. 1996. "Gubernatorial Popularity in Three States: A Preliminary Model." *Social Science Journal* 33 (1): 39–54.

Crowley, Jocelyn Elise. 2000. "Supervised Devolution: The Case of Child Support Enforcement in the United States." *Publius* 30:99–117.

Cummins, Jeff. 2009. "Issue Voting and Crime in Gubernatorial Elections." *Social Science Quarterly* 90 (3): 632–651.

Cusack, T. 1997. "Partisan Politics and Public Finance." *Public Choice* 91:375–395.

———. 1999. "Partisan Politics and Fiscal Policy." *Comparative Political Studies* 32:464–486.

———. 2000. "Partisanship in the Setting and Coordination of Fiscal and Monetary Policies." *European Journal of Political Research* 40:93–115.

Delorme, R., and C. André. 1983. *L'Etat et l'économie*. Paris: Seuil.

Derthick, Marsha. 1975a. *Policy Making for Social Security*. Washington, DC: The Brookings Institution.

———. 1975b. *Uncontrollable Spending for Social Service Grants*. Washington, DC: The Brookings Institution.

Devine, Joel A. 1985. "State and State Expenditure: Determinants of Social Investment and Social Consumption Spending in the Postwar United Sates." *American Sociological Review* 50:150–165.

Devins, Neal. 2004. "The Majoritarian Rehnquist Court?" *Law and Contemporary Problems* 67:63–81.

Digler, Robert, George Krause, and Randolph Moffett. 1995. "State Legislative Professionalism and Gubernatorial Effectiveness, 1978–1991." *Legislative Studies Quarterly* 20:553–571.

Dixit, Avinash, and John Londregan. 1996. "The Determinants of Success of Special Interests in Redistributive Politics." *Journal of Politics* 58:1132–1155.

Dometrius, Nelson C. 1979. "Measuring Gubernatorial Power." *Journal of Politics* 41:589–610.

———. 2002. "Gubernatorial Popularity and Administrative Influence." *State Politics and Policy Quarterly* 2:251–267.

Dometrius, Nelson, and Deil Wright. 2010. "Governors, Legislatures, and State Budgets across Time." *Political Research Quarterly* 63:783–795.

Due, John F., and John L. Mikesell. 1994. *Sales Taxation, State and Local Structure, and Administration*. 2nd ed. Washington, DC: Urban Institute Press.

Dye, Thomas. 1966. *Politics, Economics, and the Public: Policy Outcomes in the American States*. Chicago: Rand McNally.

———. 1969. "Executive Power and Public Policy in the States." *Western Political Quarterly* 27:926–939.

Edwards, George, and Stephen Wayne. 1990. *Presidential Leadership: Politics and Policy Making*. Boston: Wadsworth Cengage Learning.

Elazar, D. J. 1998. "State-Local Relations: Union and Home Rule." In *Governing Partners: State-Local Relations in the U.S.*, ed. Russell L. Hanson, 37–52. Boulder, CO: Westview Press.

Ellis, C. J., and M. A. Thomas. 1991. "Causality in Political Business Cycles." *Contemporary Economic Policy* 9:39–49.

Ellwood, John, and Joshua Guetzkow. 2009. "Footing the Bill: Causes and Budgetary Consequences of State Spending on Corrections." In *Do Prisons Make Us Safer? The Benefits and Costs of the Prison Boom*, ed. Steven Raphael and Michael Stoll. New York: Russell Sage Foundation.

Erikson, Robert, Gerald Wright, and John McIver. 1989. "Political Parties, Public Opinion, and State Policy in the United States." *American Political Science Review* 83:729–750.

Fair, R. 1978. "The Effect of Economic Events on Votes for President." *Review of Economics and Statistics* 60:159–172.

———. 1982. "The Effect of Economic Events on Votes for President: 1980 Results." *Rev. Econ. Stat.* 64:322–325.

———. 1988. "The Effect of Economic Events on Votes for President: 1984 Update." *Political Behavior* 10:168–179.

Farah, Barbara G., and Ethel Klein. 1989. "Public Opinion Trends." In *The Election of 1988: Reports and Interpretations*, ed. Gerald Pomper. Chatham: Chatham House.

Feld, Lars, and Christoph Schaltegger. 2005. "Voters as a Hard Budget Constraint: On the Determination of Intergovernmental Grants." *Public Choice* 123:147–169.

Feldman, Len. 2010. "CTA-Opposed Race to the Top Bills Enacted." *Educator* 15:1. http://www.cta.org/en/Professional-Development/Publications/2010/02/Educator-Feb-10/CTA-opposed-RTTT-bills-enacted.aspx.

Fenno, Richard, Jr. 1973. *Congressmen in Committees*. Boston: Little, Brown.

Ferguson, Margaret. 2003. "Chief Executive Success in the Legislative Arena." *State Politics and Policy Quarterly* 3:158–182.

Fett, Patrick. 1994. "Presidential Legislative Priorities and Legislators' Voting Decisions: An Exploratory Analysis." *Journal of Politics* 56:502–512.

Finkel, Steven E. 1993. "Reexamining the 'Minimal Effects' Model in Recent Presidential Campaigns." *Journal of Politics* 55:1–21.

Fiorina, Morris P. 1977. "An Outline for a Model of Party Choice." *American Journal of Political Science* 21 (3): 601–625.

———. 1984. "Flagellating the Federal Bureaucracy." In *The Political Economy*, ed. Thomas Ferguson and Joel Rogers, 224–234. Armonk, NY: M. E. Sharpe.

Fording, Richard C. 2010. "Laboratories of Democracy or Symbolic Politics?" In *Race and the Politics of Welfare Reform*, ed. Sanford F. Schram, Joe Brian Soss, and Richard Carl Fording. Ann Arbor: University of Michigan Press.

Fording, Richard C., Neal D. Woods, and David Prince. 2002. "Explaining Gubernatorial Success in State Legislatures." 2nd Annual Conference on State Politics and Policy: Legislatures and Representation in the United States, University of Wisconsin, Milwaukee, May.

Fossett, J. W. 1983. *Federal Aid to Big Cities: The Politics of Dependence.* Washington, DC: Brookings Institution.

———. 1987. "The Consequences of Shifting Control: Federal and State Distribution of Small Cities CDBG Funds in Four Southern States." *Publius* 17 (4): 65–80.

Fossett, J. W., and N. Richard. 1979. "Urban Conditions: The Future of the Federal Role." Paper presented at the 71st Convention of the National Tax Association, Columbus, Ohio.

Fouda, S. M. 1997. "Political Monetary Cycles and Independence of the Central Bank in a Monetary Union: An Empirical Test for a BEAC Franc Zone Member." *Journal of African Economics* 6:112–131.

Franzese, R. J. 1999. "Partially Independent Central Banks, Politically Responsive Governments, and Inflation." *American Journal of Political Science* 43:681–706.

———. 2002a. *Macroeconomic Policies of Developed Democracies.* Cambridge, UK: Cambridge University Press.

———. 2002b. "Multiple Hands on the Wheel: Empirically Modeling Partial Delegation and Shared Control of Monetary Policy in the Open and Institutionalized Economy." Department of Political Science, University of Michigan, Ann Arbor. http://www-personal.umich.edu/~franzese/CB.ER.IE.Submission.pdf.

———. 2002c. "Strategic Interactions of Monetary Policymakers and Wage/Price Bargainers: A Review with Implications for the European Common-Currency Area." *Empirical Journal of Applied Economics and Economic Policy* 28:458–486.

Frey, Bruno S., and Friedrich Schneider. 1978a. "A Politico-economic Model of the United Kingdom." *Economic Journal* 88:243–253.

———. 1978b. "An Empirical Study of Politico-economic Interaction in the United States." *Review of Economics and Statistics* 60:174–183.

———. 1979. "An Econometric Model with an Endogenous Government Sector." *Public Choice* 34:29–43.

Gais, Thomas, and James Fossett. 2005. "Federalism and the Executive Branch." In *The Executive Branch,* ed. Joel D. Aberbach and Mark A. Peterson, 486–522. New York: Oxford University Press.

Galvin, Daniel. 2009. *Presidential Party Building.* Princeton, NJ: Princeton University Press.

Gamkhar, Shama, and Hamid Ali. 2008. "Political Economy of Grant Allocations: The Case of Federal Highway Demonstration Grants," *Publius* 38:1–21.

Gamkhar, Shama, and Wallace Oates. 1996. "Asymmetries in the Response to Increases and Decreases in Intergovernmental Grants: Some Empirical Findings." *National Tax Journal* 49 (4): 501–512.

Garrett, G. 1995. "Capital Mobility, Trade, and the Domestic Politics of Economic Policy." *International Organizations* 49:657–687.

———. 1998. *Partisan Politics in the Global Economy.* Cambridge, UK: Cambridge University Press.

Gerber, Brian, Cherie Maestras, and Nelson Dometrius. 2005. "State Legislative Influence over Agency Rulemaking: The Utility of Ex Ante Review." *State Politics and Policy Quarterly* 5:24–46.

Gimpel, James G. 1998. "Packing Heat at the Polls: Gun Ownership, Interest Group Endorsements, and Voting Behavior in Gubernatorial Elections." *Social Science Quarterly* 79 (3): 634–648.

Girard, F. 2004. "Global Implications of U.S. Domestic and International Policies on Sexuality." IWGSSP Working papers, No. 1.

Gleiber, Dennis, and Stephen Shull. 1992. "Presidential Influence in the Policymaking Process." *Western Political Quarterly* 45:441–467.

Glied, Sherry, and Stephanie Ma. 2013. "How States Stand to Gain or Lose Federal Funds by Opting In or Out of the Medicaid Expansion." *The Common Wealth Fund: Issue Brief* 32:1–12.

Goetz, C. J., and C. R. McKnew. 1972. "Paradoxical Results in a Public Choice Model of Alternative Government Grant Forms." In *The Theory of Public Choice: Essays in Application*, ed. J. M. Buchanan and R. S. Tollison, 189–224. Ann Arbor: University of Michigan Press.

Golden, David, and James Poterba. 1980. "The Price of Popularity: The Political Business Cycle Reexamined." *American Journal of Political Science* 24:696–714.

Gonzalez, M. A. 1999a. "On Elections, Democracy, and Macroeconomic Policy Cycles." Working paper. Department of Economics, Princeton University.

———. 1999b. "Political Budget Cycles and Democracy: A Multi-Country Analysis." Working paper. Department of Economics, Princeton University.

———. 2000. "On Elections, Democracy, and Macroeconomic Policy: Evidence from Mexico." Working paper. Department of Economics, Princeton University.

Gordon, N. 2004. "Do Federal Grants Boost School Spending? Evidence from Title I." *Journal of Public Economics* 88:1771–1792.

Gosling, James J. 1994. "Budget Procedures and Executive Review in State Legislatures." In *The Encyclopedia of American Legislatures*, ed. Joseph Silbey. New York: Scribner's.

Gramlich, Edward. 1977. "Intergovernmental Grants: A Review of the Literature." In *The Political Economy of Federalism*, ed. Wallace Oates. Lexington, MA: Lexington Books.

———. 1989. "Budget Deficits and National Saving: Are Politicians Exogenous?" *Journal of Economic Perspectives* 3:23–35.

Gramlich, Edward M., and Harvey Galper. 1973. "State and Local Fiscal Behavior and Federal Grant Policy." *Brookings Papers on Economic Activity* 4 (1): 15–65.

Greve, Michael. 1999. *Real Federalism: What It Is, Why It Matters*. New York: AEI Press.

Grodzins, Morton. 1966. "The American System: A New View of Government in the United States." Chicago: Rand McNally.

Gronke, Paul. 1999. "Policies, Prototypes, and Presidential Approval." Paper presented at the Annual Meeting of the American Political Science Association, Atlanta.

Gross, Donald A. 1991. "The Policy Role of Governors." In *Gubernatorial Leadership and State Policy*, ed. Eric B. Herzik and Brent W. Brown, 1–24. New York: Greenwood Press.

Grossman, Philip. 1994. "A Political Theory of Intergovernmental Grants." *Public Choice* 30:295–303.

Grossman, Philip J., and Edwin G. West. 1994. "Federalism and the Growth of Government Revisited." *Public Choice* 79 (1/2): 19–32.

Hahm, S. D. 1996. "The Political Economy of Deficit Spending: A Cross Comparison of Industrialized Democracies, 1955–90." *Environmental Planning* 14:227–250.

Hahm, S. D., M. Kamlet, and D. Mowery. 1996. "The Political Economy of Deficit Spending in Nine Industrialized Parliamentary Democracies: The Role of Fiscal Institutions." *Comparative Political Studies* 29:52–77.

Haider, Donald. 1974. *When Governments Come to Washington: Governors, Mayors, and Intergovernmental Lobbying.* New York: Free Press.

Hallerberg, M., and S. Basinger. 1998. "Internationalization and Changes in Tax Policy in OECD Nations: The Importance of Domestic Veto Players." *Comparative Political Studies* 31:321–353.

Hallerberg, M., L. Vinhas de Souza, and W. R. Clark. 2002. "Monetary and Fiscal Cycles in EU Accession Countries." *European Union Politics* 3:231–250.

Hansen, Susan B. 1999. "Life Is Not Fair: Governors' Job Performance Ratings and State Economies." *Political Research Quarterly* 52 (1): 167–188.

Hanson, Russell L., and Michael T. Heaney. 1997. "The Silent Revolution in Welfare: AFDC Waivers during the Bush and Clinton Administrations." In *Annual Meeting of the Midwest Political Science Association, Chicago.*

Harrinvirta, M., and M. Mattila. 2001. "The Hard Business of Balancing Budgets: A Study in Public Finances in Seventeen OECD Countries." *British Journal of Political Science* 31:497–522.

Haynes, S. E., and J. Stone. 1988. "Does the Political Business Cycle Dominate U.S. Unemployment and Inflation? Some New Evidence." In *Political Business Cycles: The Political Economy of Money, Inflation, and Unemployment,* ed. Thomas Willett, 276–297. Durham, NC: Duke University Press.

———. 1989. "An Integrated Test for Electoral Cycles in the US Economy." *Review of Economics Statistics* 71:426–434.

———. 1990. "Political Models of the Business Cycle Should be Revived." *Economic Inquiry* 28:442–465.

———. 1994. "Political Parties and the Variable Duration of Business Cycles." *Southern Economics Journal* 60:869–885.

Hebert, F. T., Jeffrey Brudney, and Deil Wright. 1983. "Gubernatorial Influence and State Bureaucracy." *American Politics Research* 11:243–264.

Heckelman, J. C., and H. Berument. 1998. "Political Business Cycles and Endogenous Elections." *Southern Economics Journal* 64:987–1000.

Heclo, Hugh. 2001. "The Politics of Welfare Reform." In *The New World of Welfare,* ed. Rebecca M. Blank and Ron Haskins, 169–200. Washington, DC: Brookings Institution Press.

Hedge, David M. 1998. *Governance and the Changing American States.* Boulder, CO: Westview.

Herron, M., and B. Theodos. 2004. "Government Redistribution in the Shadow of

Legislative Elections: A Study of the Illinois Member Initiative Grants Program."
Legislative Studies Quarterly 29:287–311.

Hibbs, D. 1977. "Political Parties and Macroeconomic Policy." *American Political Science Review* 71:1467–1487.

———. 1986. "Political Parties and Macroeconomic Policies and Outcomes in the United States." *American Economic Review* 76:66–70.

———. 1987a. *The American Political Economy: Macroeconomics and Electoral Politics.* Cambridge, MA: Harvard University Press.

———. 1987b. *The Political Economy of Industrial Democracies.* Cambridge, MA: Harvard University Press.

———. 1992. "Partisan Theory after Fifteen Years." *European Journal of Political Economy* 8:361–373.

———. 1994. "The Partisan Model and Macroeconomic Cycles: More Theory and Evidence from the United States." *Economics and Politics* 6:1–24.

Hiltzik, Michael. 2014. Medicaid Expansion is the Final Battle in War over Obamacare. *Los Angeles Times,* May 4. http://www.latimes.com/business/hiltzik/la-fi-hiltzik-20140504-column.html#page=1.

Hines, James, and Richard Thaler. 1995. "Anomalies: The Flypaper Effect." *Journal of Economic Perspectives* 9:217–226.

Hoffman, Kim U. 2006. "Legislative Fiscal Analysts: Influence in State Budget Development." *State and Local Government Review* 38:41–51.

Holbrook, Thomas M., and Scott McClurg. 2005. "Presidential Campaigns and the Mobilization of Core Supporters." *American Journal of Political Science* 49:689–703.

Holsey, Cheryl M., and Thomas E. Borcherding. 1997. "Why Does Government's Share of National Income Grow? An Assessment of the Recent Literature on the U.S. Experience." In *Perspectives on Public Choice: A Handbook,* ed. Dennis C. Mueller. Cambridge: Cambridge University Press.

Houser, Ari, Wendy Fox-Grage, Mary Joe Gibson. 2006 *Across the States: Profiles of Long-term Care and Independent Living.* Washington, DC: AARP Public Policy Institute.

Howell, Susan E., and James M. Vanderleeuw. 1990. "Economic Effects on State Governors." *American Politics Research* 18 (2): 158–168.

Imbeau, L., F. Petry, and M. Lamari. 2001. "Left-Right Party Ideology and Government Policies." *European Journal of Economic Research* 40:1–29.

Ingram, Helen. 1977a. *Public Participation in Environmental Decision Making: Substance or Illusion?* New York: Wiley.

———. 1977b. "Policy Implementation through Bargaining: The Case of Federal Grants-in-Aid." *Public Policy* 25:499.

Jacobson, Gary. 1987. "The Marginals Never Vanished: Incumbency and Competition in Elections to the U.S. House of Representatives, 1952–82." *American Journal of Political Science* 31:126–141.

Jacobson, Gary, Samuel Kernell, and Jeffrey Lazarus. 2004. "The President and the Distribution of Federal Spending." *Legislative Studies Quarterly* 29:159–184.

Jacoby, William G., and Saundra K. Schneider. 2001. "Variability in State Policy Priorities: An Empirical Analysis." *Journal of Politics* 63:544–568.

Jensen, Jennifer M., and Thad Beyle. 2003. "Of Footnotes, Missing Data, and Lessons for 50-State Data Collection: The Gubernatorial Campaign Finance Data Project, 1977–2001." *State Politics and Policy Quarterly* 3 (2): 203–214.

Jessee, Stephen A. 2010. "Partisan Bias, Political Information and Spatial Voting in the 2008 Presidential Election." *Journal of Politics* 72 (2): 327–340.

Jonsson, G. 1995. "Institutions and Macroeconomic Outcomes—The Empirical Evidence." *Swedish Economic and Policy Review* 2:181–212.

Kaiser Commission on Medicaid and the Uninsured. 2011. *Five Key Questions and Answers about Section 1115 Medicaid Demonstration Waivers*, June. http://kaiserfamily foundation.files.wordpress.com/2013/01/8196.pdf.

Kaiser Health News. 2011. "Harkin Blasts South Carolina over Exchange Grant." *Kaiser Health News*, Dec. 23. http://www.kaiserhealthnews.org/daily-reports/2011/de cember/23/south-carolina-exchange-grant.aspx.

Keech, W., and K. Pak. 1983. "Electoral Cycles and Budgetary Growth in Veterans' Benefits Programs." *American Journal of Political Science* 33:901–911.

Kenney, Patrick J. 1983. "The Effect of State Economic Conditions on the Vote for Governor." *Social Science Quarterly* 64:154–162.

Kenney, Patrick J., and Tom W. Rice. 1983. "Popularity and the Vote: The Gubernatorial Case." *American Politics Quarterly* 11:237–241.

Khemani, S. 2000. "Political Cycles in a Developing Economy: Effect of Elections in the Indian States." Working paper. World Bank. http://wbln0018.worldbank.org/ Research/workpapers.nsf/5ade973899c860868525673106834d5/0bd238deeb3b8f 1f852569600052bc35/$FILE/wps2454.pdf.

Kiewiet, Roderick, and Mathew McCubbins. 1985. "Congressional Appropriations and the Electoral Connection." *Journal of Politics* 47:59–82.

King, Anthony. 1983. *Both Ends of the Avenue: The Presidency, the Executive Branch, and Congress in the 1980s*. Washington, DC: American Enterprise Institute.

King, James D. 2001. "Incumbent Popularity and Vote Choice in Gubernatorial Elections." *Journal of Politics* 63 (2): 585–597.

Kingdon, J. W. 1984. *Agendas, Alternatives and Public Policies*. New York: Pearson.

Knight, B. 2002. "Endogenous Federal Grants and Crowd-out of State Government Spending: Theory and Evidence from the Federal Highway Aid Program." *American Economic Review* 92:71–92.

Kousser, Thad, and Justin Phillips. 2012. *The Power of American Governors*. New York: Cambridge University Press.

Krane, Dale. 1987. "Devolution of the Small Cities CDBG Program in Mississippi." *Publius* 17 (4): 81–96.

———. 1993. "American Federalism, State Governments, and Public Policy." *PS: Political Science and Politics* 26:186–190.

Krause, George, David Lewis, and James Douglas. 2006. "Political Appointments, Civil Service Systems, and Bureaucratic Competence: Organizational Balancing and Executive Branch Revenue Forecasts in the American States." *American Journal of Political Science* 50:770–787.

Krueger, A., and I. Turan. 1993. "The Politics and Economics of Turkish Policy Reform in the 1980s." In *Political and Economic Interactions in Economic Policy Reform: Evidence from Eight Countries*, ed. R. Bates. Cambridge: Blackwell.

Lachler, U. 1978. "The Political Business Cycle: A Complimentary Study." *Review of Economic Studies* 45:131–143.

———. 1982. "On Political Business Cycles with Endogenous Election Dates." *Journal of Public Economics* 17:111–117.

Larcinese, Valentino, Leonzio Rizzo, and Cecelia Testa. 2006. "Allocating the U.S. Federal Budget to the States: The Impact of the President." *Journal of Politics* 68:447–456.

Lees-Marshment, Jennifer. 2001. "The Marriage of Politics and Marketing." *Political Studies* 49:692–713.

Levernier, William. 1992. "The Effect of Relative Economic Performance on the Outcome of Gubernatorial Elections." *Public Choice* 74 (2): 181–190.

Levitt, Steven D., and James M. Snyder Jr. 1995. "Political Parties and the Distribution of Federal Outlays." *American Journal of Political Science* 39:958–980.

Lewis-Beck, Michael S. 1988. *Economics and Elections: The Major Western Democracies.* Ann Arbor: University of Michigan Press.

Lewis-Beck, Michael S., and Martin Paldam. 2000. "Economic Voting: An Introduction." *Electoral Studies* 19 (2): 113–121.

Leyden, Kevin M., and Stephen A. Borrelli. 1995. "The Effect of State Economic Conditions on Gubernatorial Elections: Does Unified Government Make a Difference?" *Political Research Quarterly* 49 (June): 275–290.

Liebschutz, Sarah F., Irene Lurie, and Richard W. Small. 1983. "How State Responses Confound Federal Policy: Reaganomics and the New Federalism in New York." *Publius* 31:51–63.

Lindbeck, Assar, and W. Jörgen Weibull. 1993. "A Model of Political Equilibrium in a Representative Democracy." *Journal of Public Economics* 51:195–209.

Logan, R. 1986. "Fiscal Illusion and the Grantor Government." *Journal of Political Economy* 94:1304–1318.

Lohmann, S. 1998. "Rationalizing the Political Business Cycle: A Workhorse Model." *Economics and Politics* 10:1–17.

———. 1999. "What Price Accountability? The Lucas Island Model and the Politics of Monetary Policy." *American Journal of Political Science* 43:396–430.

Lowi, T. J. 1977. "Public Policy and Bureaucracy in the United States and France." Paper presented at the Meeting of International Political Science Association, Edinburgh. Published in *Comparing Public Policies*, ed. Douglas Ashford. New York: Sage.

Lowrey, Robert C., James Alt, and Karen Ferree. 1998. "Fiscal Policy Outcomes and Electoral Accountability in the States." *American Political Science Review* 92:759–774.

MacDonald, Jason A., and Lee Sigelman. 1999. "Public Assessments of Gubernatorial Performance: A Comparative State Analysis." *American Politics Research* 27 (2): 201–215.

Macdonald, Stuart Elaine, George Rabinowitz, and Ola Listhaug. 1995. "Political Sophistication and Models of Issue Voting." *British Journal of Political Science* 25:453–483.

MacRae, C. D. 1977. "A Political Model of the Business Cycle." *Journal of Political Economy* 85:239–263.

Malaby, M., and D. Webber. 1991. "Federalism in the 101st Congress." *Publius* 21:77–92.

Maloney, H., and M. Smirlock. 1981. "Business Cycles and the Political Process." *Southern Economics Journal* 47:377–392.

Martin, Brent. 2011. "Heineman and Nelson Exchange Words over Health Exchanges." *Nebraska Radio Network.* http://nebraskaradionetwork.com/2011/12/08/heineman-and-nelson-exchange-words-over-health-exchanges-audio.

Mayhew, David. 1974. *Congress: The Electoral Connection.* New Haven: Yale University Press.

McAtee, Andrea, Susan Webb Yackee, and David Lowery. 2003. "Reexamining the Dynamic Model of Divided Partisan Government." *Journal of Politics* 65:477–490.

McCallum, B. 1978. "The Political Business Cycle: An Empirical Test." *Southern Economics Journal* 44:504–515.

McGuire, M. 1975. "An Econometric Model of Federal Grants and Local Fiscal Response." In *Financing the New Federalism*, ed. Wallace Oates, 115–139. Baltimore: RFF Press.

Megdal, Shannon Bernstein. 1987. "The Flypaper Effect Revisited: An Econometric Explanation." *Review of Economics and Statistics* 69:347–351.

Metz, Cara. 2010. "Panel Looks at Pros and Cons of Race to the Top," *New York Teacher.* http://www.nysut.org/newyorkteacher_14714.htm.

Mikesell, John. 2007. "Changing State Fiscal Capacity and Tax Effort in an Era of Devolving Government, 1981–2003." *Publius* 37:532–550.

Milligan, Kevin, and Michael Smart. 2005. "Regional Grants as Pork Barrel Politics." CESifo Working Paper Series No. 1453. http://ssrn.com/abstract=710903.

Morehouse, Sarah. 1981. *State Politics, Parties, and Policy.* New York: Holt.

———. 1996. "Legislative Party Voting for the Governor's Program." *Legislative Studies Quarterly* 21:359–381.

———. 1998. *The Governor as Party Leader: Campaigning and Governing.* Ann Arbor: University of Michigan Press.

Moyo, D. 1999. "The Determinants of Public Savings in Developing Countries." Working paper. Department of Economics, Oxford University.

Mueller, Dennis. 2003. *Public Choice III.* New York: Cambridge University Press.

Mueller, K. J. 1985. "Explaining Variation and Change in Gubernatorial Powers, 1960–1982." *Western Political Quarterly* 38:424–431.

Nathan, Richard. 1983. *The Administrative Presidency.* New York: John Wiley and Sons Inc.

Nathan, Richard, and Fred Doolittle. 1984. "The Untold Story of Reagan's New Federalism." *The Public Interest* 77:96–105.

———. 1985. "Federal Grants: Giving and Taking Away." *Political Science Quarterly* 100:53–74.

Needham, Catherine. 2005. "Brand Leaders: Clinton, Blair and the Limitations of the Permanent Campaign." *Political Studies* 53 (2): 343–361.

Neustadt, Richard. 1980. "US Privacy Policy—A Comprehensive Programme." *Telecommunications Policy* 4:64–65.

Nice, David C. 1987. *Federalism: The Politics of Intergovernmental Relations.* New York: St. Martins Press.

Nicholson-Crotty, Sean. 2004. "Goal Conflict and Fund Diversion in Federal Grants to the States." *American Journal of Political Science* 48:110–122.

———. 2009. "The Politics of Diffusion: Public Policy in the American States." *Journal of Politics* 71:192–205.

———. 2012. "Leaving Money on the Table: Learning from Recent Refusals of Federal Grants in the American States." *Publius* 42:449–466.

Nicholson-Crotty, Sean, and Tucker Staley. 2012. "Competitive Federalism and Race to the Top Application Decisions in the American States." *Educational Policy* 26:160–184.

Nicholson-Crotty, Sean, Tucker Staley, and Mark Ritchey. 2011. "Integrating Models of Competitive Federalism: The Case of Gubernatorial Credit Claiming." Presented at the Annual Meeting of the Midwest Political Science Association, Chicago, March 31–April 4.

Nicholson-Crotty, Sean, and Nick Theobald. 2010. "Claiming Credit in the U.S. Federal System: Testing a Model of Competitive Federalism." *Publius.* First published online October 11. doi:10.1093/publius/pjq029 31.

Nicholson-Crotty, Sean, Nick Theobald, and B. Dan Wood. 2006. "Fiscal Federalism and Budgetary Tradeoffs in the American States." *Political Research Quarterly* 59:313–321.

Niemi, Richard G., Harold W. Stanley, and Ronald J. Vogel. 1995. "State Economies and State Taxes: Do Voters Hold Governors Accountable?" *American Journal of Political Science* 39:936–957.

Nordhaus, W. D. 1975. "The Political Business Cycle." *Review of Economic Studies* 42:169–190.

Oates, Wallace E. 1979. "Lump-Sum Intergovernmental Grants Have Price Effects." *Fiscal Federalism and Grants-in-aid* 23:30–41.

———. 1991. *Studies in Fiscal Federalism.* Northampton, MA: Edward Elgar Publishing.

Oates, Wallace, and D. Bradford. 1971. "Towards a Predictive Theory of Intergovernmental Grants." *American Economic Review* 61:440–448.

Oatley, T. 1993. "How Constraining Is Capital Mobility? The Partisan Hypothesis in an Open Economy." *American Journal of Political Science* 43:1003–1027.

Oberg, Jon. 1997. "Testing Federal Student-Aid Fungibility in Two Competing Versions of Federalism." *Publius* 27:115–134.

O'Brien, David. 1993. "The Rehnquist Court and Federal Preemption: In Search of a Theory." *Publius* 23:15–32.

Orth, Deborah A. 2001. "Accountability in a Federal System: The Governor, the President, and Economic Expectations." *State Politics and Policy Quarterly* 1 (4): 412–432.

Partin, Randall W. 1995. "Economic Conditions and Gubernatorial Elections: Is the State Executive Held Accountable?" *American Politics Research* 23 (1): 81–95.

———. 2002. "Assessing the Impact of Campaign Spending in Governors' Races." *Political Research Quarterly* 55 (1): 213–233.

Peltzman, Sam. 1987. "Economic Conditions and Gubernatorial Elections." *American Economic Review* 77:293–297.

Peterson, Paul. 1981. *City Limits.* Chicago: University of Chicago Press.

———. 1995. *The Price of Federalism.* Washington, DC: The Brookings Institution.

Petrocik, John R. 1996. "Issue Ownership in Presidential Elections, with a 1980 Case Study." *American Journal of Political Science* 40:825–850.

Petry, F., L. M. Imbeau, J. Crete, and M. Clavet. 1999. "Electoral and Partisan Cycles in the Canadian Provinces." *Canadian Journal of Political Science* 32:273–292.

Pew Charitable Trust. 2014. *State Spending on Medicaid.* http://www.pewtrusts.org/~/media/Data-Visualizations/Interactives/2014/Medicaid/downloadables/State_Health_Care_Spending_on_Medicaid.pdf.

Posner, Eric. 1996. "The Regulation of Groups: The Influence of Legal and Nonlegal Sanctions on Collective Action." *University of Chicago Law Review* 63:133–197.

Posner, Paul. 1998. *The Politics of Unfunded Mandates: Whither Federalism?* Washington, DC: Georgetown University Press.

Posner, Paul, and Margaret Wrightson. 1996. "*Block Grants:* A Perennial, But Unstable Tool of Government." *Publius* 26:87–108.

Prakash, Saikrishna. 2002. "Are the Judicial Safeguards of Federalism the Ultimate Form of Conservative Judicial Activism?" *University of Colorado Law Review* 73:1363–1382.

Prakash, Saikrishna, and Yoo John Choon. 2001. "The Puzzling Persistence of Process-Based Federalism Theories." *Texas Law Review.* http://ssrn.com/abstract=268862 or http://dx.doi.org/10.2139/ssrn.268862.

Price, S. 1998. "Comment on 'The Politics of the Political Business Cycle.'" *British Journal of Political Science* 28:201–210.

Renaud, P., and F. van Winden. 1987. "On the Importance of Elections and Ideology for Government Policy in a Multi-party System." In *The Logic of Multiparty Systems,* ed. M. J. Holler. Dordrecht: Kluwer Academic Publisher.

Rich, Michael. 1989. "Distributive Politics and the Allocation of Federal Grants." *American Political Science Review* 83:193–213.

Riffe, D., S. Lacy, and F. G. Fico. 2005. *Analyzing Media Messages: Using Quantitative Content Analysis in Research.* 2nd ed. Mahwah, NJ: Lawrence Erlbaum Associates.

Ringquist, Evan, and James Garand. 1999. "Policy Change in the American States." In *American State and Local Politics,* ed. Ronald E. Weber and Paul Brace. New York: Chatham House.

Rodden, Jonathan. 2006. *Hamilton's Paradox: The Promise and Peril of Fiscal Federalism.* Cambridge: Cambridge University Press.

Rogoff, K. 1990. "Equilibrium Political Budget Cycles." *American Economics Review* 80:21–36.

Rogoff, K., and A. Sibert. 1988. "Elections and Macroeconomic Policy Cycles." *Review of Economic Studies* 55:1–16.

Romer, Thomas, and Howard Rosenthal. 1980. "An Institutional Theory of the Effect of Intergovernmental Grants." *National Tax Journal* 33:451–459.

Rosenthal, Alan. 1990. *Governors and Legislatures: Contending Powers.* Washington, DC: CQ Press.

———. 1998. *The Decline of Democracy.* Washington DC: CQ Press.

Ross, F. 1997. "Cutting Public Expenditures in Advanced Industrial Democracies: The Importance of Avoiding Blame." *Governance: International Journal of Policy Administration* 10:175–200.

Rothschild, Scott. 2011. "Brownback Says State Is Returning to Feds $31.5 Million Health Care Reform Grant." *Tonganoxie Mirror,* August 10. http://www.tongan oxiemirror.com/news/2011/aug/10/brownback-says-state-returning-feds-315-mil lion-he/?print.

Rundquist, Barry S., and Thomas M. Carsey. 2002. *Congress and Defense Spending: The Distributive Politics of Military Procurement.* Norman: University of Oklahoma Press.

Sack, Kevin. 2011. "Opposing the Health Law, Florida Refuses Millions." *New York Times,* July 31. http://www.nytimes.com/2011/08/01/us/01florida.html?pagewanted =all&_r=0.

Schneider, Saundra. 1989. "Governors and Health Care Policymaking: The Case of Medicaid." In *Gubernatorial Leadership and State Policy,* ed. Eric B. Herzik and Brent W. Brown. New York: Greenwood Press.

Schneider, Saundra K., and William G. Jacoby. 1996. "Influences on Bureaucratic Policy Initiatives in the American States." *Journal of Public Administration Research and Theory* 6 (4): 495–522.

Schuknecht, L. 1999. "Fiscal Policy Cycles and the Exchange Rate Regime in Developing Countries." *European Journal of Political Economy* 15:569–580.

———. 2000. "Fiscal Policy Cycles and Public Expenditure in Developing Countries." *Public Choice* 102:115–130.

Schultz, K. A. 1995. "The Politics of the Political Business Cycle." *British Journal of Political Science* 25:79–99.

Sharkansky, Ira. 1968. "Agency Requests, Gubernatorial Support, and Budget Success in State Legislatures." *American Political Science Review* 26:1220–1231.

Sheffrin, S. 1989. "Evaluating Rational Partisan Business Cycle Theory." *Economics and Politics* 1:239–259.

Shi, M., and J. Svensson. 2001. "Conditional Political Budget Cycles." Working paper. University of Wisconsin and Institute for International Economic Studies, Stockholm University. http://www.iies.su.se/»svenssoj/pbc.pdf.

Sieg, G. 1997. "A Model of Partisan Central Banks and Opportunistic Political Business Cycles." *European Journal of Political Economics* 13:503–516.

Sigelman, Lee, and Nelson Dometrius. 1988. "Modeling the Impact of Supreme Court Decisions: *Wygant v. Board.*" *Journal of Politics* 50:131–149.

Simmons, B. 1996. "Rulers of the Game: Central Bank Independence during the Interwar Years." *International Organizations* 50:407–443.

Sims, Edward. 1961. "U.S. Housing Aid Feared Forced Integration Step." *Sunday Independent*, April 9.

Smith, Steven S., and Christopher J. Deering. 1984. *Committees in Congress.* Washington, DC: Congressional Quarterly Press.

Sobel, Russell. 1998. "The Political Economy of Conflict and Appropriation." *Public Choice* 95:210–213.

Society for Adolescent Medicine. 2006. "Abstinence-only Policies and Programs: A Position Paper of the Society for Adolescent Medicine." *Journal of Adolescent Health* 38:83–87.

Soss, Joe, Sanford F. Schram, Thomas P. Vartanian, and Erin O'Brien. 2001. "Setting the Terms of Relief: Explaining State Policy Choices in the Devolution Revolution." *American Journal of Political Science* 45:378–395.

Squire, Peverill. 2007. "Measuring State Legislative Professionalism: The Squire Index Revisited." *State Politics and Policy Quarterly* 7 (2):211–227.

Stein, Robert. 1981. "The Allocation of Federal Aid Monies: The Synthesis of Demand-Side and Supply-Side Explanations." *American Political Science Review* 75:334–343.

———. 1990. "Economic Voting for Governor and U.S. Senator: The Consequences of Federalism." *Journal of Politics* 52:29–53.

———. 2010. "Health Bill Restores $250 Million in Abstinence-Education Funds." *Washington Post*, March 27. http://www.washingtonpost.com/wp-dyn/content/ar ticle/2010/03/26/ AR2010032602457.html. Accessed April 13, 2012.

Stigler, G. 1973. "General Economic Conditions and National Elections." *American Economics Review* 63:160–167.

Stonecash, Jeff. 1981. "Centralization in State-Local Fiscal Relationships." *Western Political Quarterly* 34:301–309.

———. 1983. "Fiscal Centralization in the American States: Increasing Similarity and Persisting Diversity." *Publius* 13:123–137.

Stuckey, T. D., and K. Heimer. 2007. "A Bigger Piece of the Pie? State Corrections Spending and the Politics of Social Order." *Journal of Research in Crime and Delinquency* 44:91–123.

Stults, Brian G., and Richard F. Winters. 2005. "The Political Economy of Taxes and the Vote." Unpublished manuscript. http://www.dartmouth.edu/~rwinters/BS% 26RW2005.pdf.

Svoboda, Craig J. 1995. "Retrospective Voting in Gubernatorial Elections: 1982 and 1986." *Political Research Quarterly* 48 (1):135–150.

Swank, D. H. 1992. "Politics and the Structural Dependence of the State in Democratic Capitalist Nations." *American Political Science Review* 86:38–54.

Tannenwald, Robert. 1999. "Fiscal Disparity Revisited." *New England Economic Review*, July–August:3–25.

Tellier, Genevieve. 2006. "Public Expenditures in Canadian Provinces: An Empirical Study of Politico-Economic Interactions." *Public Choice* 126:367–385.

Thompson, Frank J., and Courtney Burke. 2007. "Executive Federalism and Medicaid Demonstration Waivers: Implications for Policy and Democratic Process." *Journal of Health Politics, Policy and Law* 32:971–1004.

———. 2008. "Federalism by Waiver: MEDICAID and the Transformation of Long-term Care." *Publius* 39:22–46.

Thompson, W., and G. Zuck. 1983. "American Elections and International Electoral-Economic Cycles: A Test of the Tufte Hypothesis." *American Journal of Political Science* 77:364–374.

Thurmaier, Kurt M., and Katherine G. Willoughby. 2001. *Policy and Politics in State Budgeting*. Armonk, NY: M. E. Sharpe.

Tomz, Michael, Jason Wittenberg, and Gary King. 2004. "2001+ CLARIFY: Software for Interpreting and Presenting Statistical Results Version 2.0." Cambridge, MA: Harvard University. Updated version available at http://gking.Harvard.edu.

Trenholm, C., B. Devaney, J. Wheeler, K. Fortson, L. Quay, and M. Clark. 2007. *Impacts of Four Title V, Section 510 Abstinence Education programs: Final Report*. Trenton, NJ: Mathematica Policy Research.

Tsebelis, George. 2002. *Veto Players: How Political Institutions Work*. Princeton, NJ: Princeton University Press.

Tufte, E. 1978. *Political Control of the Economy*. Princeton, NJ: Princeton University Press.

Turnbull, Geoffrey K. 1998. "The Overspending and Flypaper Effects of Fiscal Illusion: Theory and Empirical Evidence." *Journal of Urban Economics* 44 (1):1–26.

U.S. General Accounting Office. 1996. "FEDERAL GRANTS—Design Improvements Could Help Federal Resources Go Further." Report to the Chairman, Committee on the Budget, House of Representatives, #AIMD-97-7.

———. 2004. "FEDERAL-AID HIGHWAYS Trends, Effect on State Spending and Options for Future Program Design." Report to the Ranking Minority Member, Subcommittee on Transportation and Infrastructure, Committee on Environment and Public Works, U.S. Senate, #GAO-4-802.

———. 2008. "Medicaid: CMS Needs More Information on the Billions of Dollars Spent on Supplemental Payments." Report #GAO-08-614.

———. 2009. "Funding for the Largest Federal Assistance Programs Is Based on Census Related Data and Other Factors." Report #GAO-10-263.

———. 2010a. "Child Care: Multiple Factors Could Have Contributed to the Recent Decline in the Number of Children Whose Families Receive Subsidies." Report # GAO-10-344.

———. 2010b. "Recovery Act: Opportunities to Improve Management and Strengthen Accountability over States' and Localities' Uses of Funds." Report #GAO-10-999.

———. 2011. "STATE AND LOCAL GOVERNMENTS: Knowledge of Past Recessions Can Inform Future Federal Fiscal Assistance." Report #GAO-11-401.

Vaubel, R. 1997. "The Bureaucratic and Partisan Behavior of Independent Central Banks: German and International Evidence." *European Journal of Political Economy* 13:201–224.

Volden, Craig. 1999. "Asymmetric Effects of Intergovernmental Grants: Analysis and Implications for U.S. Welfare Policy." *Publius* 29:51–73.

———. 2005. "Intergovernmental Political Competition in American Federalism." *American Journal of Political Science* 49:327–342.

———. 2007. "Intergovernmental grants: A formal model of interrelated national and subnational political decisions." *Publius* 32:209–243.

Walker, David B. 2000. *The Rebirth of Federalism*. New York: Chatham House Publishers.

Way, C. 2000. "Central Banks, Partisan Politics, and Macroeconomic Outcomes." *Comparative Political Studies* 33:196–224.

Weaver, R. Kent. 1996. "Deficits and Devolution in the 104th Congress." *Publius* 26 (3): 45–86.

Weaver, R., P. Freund, and J. Wright. 1968. *The Future of Federalism*. Detroit, MI: Wayne State University Press.

Wechsler, Herbert. 1954. "Political Safeguards of Federalism: The Role of the States in the Composition and Selection of the National Government." *Columbia Law Review* 54:543.

Weissert, C. S., and W. G. Weissert. 2006. "Medicaid Waivers: License to Shape the Future of Fiscal Federalism." Paper presented at the Annual Meeting of the American Political Science Association, Philadelphia, Sept. 1–3.

Wilde, J. A. 1968. "The Expenditure Effects of Grant-in-Aid Programs." *National Tax Journal* 21:340–348.

Wohlenberg, Ernest. 1992. "Recent U.S. Gambling Legislation: A Study of Lotteries." *Social Science Journal* 29:167–183.

Woods, Neal. 2004. "Political Influence on Agency Rulemaking: Examining Effects on Legislative and Gubernatorial Rule Review Powers." *State and Local Government Review* 36:174–185.

Wright, G. 1974. "The Political Economy of New Deal Spending: An Econometric Analysis." *Review of Economics and Statistics* 56:30–39.

Yoo, J. C. 1996. "The Judicial Safeguard of Federalism." *Southern California Law Review* 70:1311.

Zimmerman, Joseph. 1991. "Federal Preemption under Reagan's New Federalism." *Publius* 21:7–28.

———. 1992. *Contemporary American Federalism: The Growth of National Power.* New York: Praeger.

———. 1996. *Interstate Relations: The Neglected Dimension of Federalism.* Westport, CT: Praeger.

———. 2005. *Congressional Preemption: Regulatory Federalism.* New York: State University of New York Press.

Index

Page numbers in italics indicate figures and tables.